TEACHERS VERSUS
THE PUBLIC

TEACHERS VERSUS THE PUBLIC

WHAT AMERICANS THINK ABOUT SCHOOLS AND HOW TO FIX THEM

Paul E. Peterson, Michael Henderson,
and Martin R. West

BROOKINGS INSTITUTION PRESS
Washington, D.C.

Copyright © 2014
THE BROOKINGS INSTITUTION
1775 Massachusetts Avenue, N.W., Washington, D.C. 20036
www.brookings.edu

Library of Congress Cataloging-in-Publication data
Peterson, Paul E., author.
  Teachers versus the public : what Americans think about their schools and
how to fix them / Paul E. Peterson, Michael B. Henderson, and Martin R. West.
      p.   cm.
  Includes bibliographical references and index.
  ISBN 978-0-8157-2552-7 (pbk. : alk. paper)
  1. Education—United States—Public opinion. 2. Educational change—
United States—Public opinion. 3. Schools—United States—Public opinion.
4. Educational surveys—United States. I. Henderson, Michael B., author.
II. West, Martin R., author. III. Title.
  LA230.P48 2014
  370.973—dc23   2013047245

9 8 7 6 5 4 3 2 1

Printed on acid-free paper

Typeset in Sabon

Composition by R. Lynn Rivenbark
Macon, Georgia

Printed by R. R. Donnelley
Harrisonburg, Virginia

To the memory of

PETER M. FLANIGAN

Contents

Contents

Preface

THE CENTRAL CONFLICT in twenty-first-century school politics—and the central theme of this short book—is perfectly captured by the photo displayed on its cover. Led by the Wisconsin Education Association, hundreds of demonstrating teachers and their allies occupy in 2012 the state's most prominent public space, the rotunda of the Wisconsin State Capitol, in an attempt to block looming legislation limiting the collective bargaining rights of certain public sector unions. By surveying the opinions of the nation's teaching force as well as those of a nationally representative sample of the general public, *Teachers versus the Public* provides a window on the size and shape of the conflict between those who work in public schools and those whom the public schools are expected to serve.

Public opinion polls are pervasive, education policy books abound, and surveys of teachers are hardly unknown, but we offer here the first systematic comparison of the education policy views of nationally representative samples of both teachers and the public as a whole. We find a deep, broad divide between the opinions held by the public and those who teach in the public schools.

We also provide the first experimental study of public and teacher opinion. Using a recently developed research strategy, we ask differently worded questions about the same topic to randomly chosen segments of our sample. This approach allows us to identify the impact on public opinion of new information on issues such as student performance and school expenditures in each respondent's community.

Under the auspices of the Harvard Program on Education Policy and Governance (PEPG) and *Education Next: A Journal of Opinion and*

Research (Ednext), we have conducted nationally representative surveys of the general public annually for seven years (2007–13) and nationally representative surveys of teachers for six years (2008–13). In 2011 the survey was administered to over 5,000 respondents, allowing us to ascertain fairly precisely the opinions of specific groups of interest within the population, such as teachers, parents, African Americans, and Hispanic Americans. Paul E. Peterson had overall responsibility for the surveys. William G. Howell was the survey director and is a co-author of chapter 6. Martin R. West played a major role in the design of each questionnaire, and Michael Henderson and Matthew Chingos played major roles in the geocoding of data and data analysis.

An undertaking this complex and costly requires financial assistance from multiple sources. The annual *Ednext* survey has been supported by the Lynde and Harry Bradley Foundation, Bill and Melinda Gates Foundation, Kern Family Foundation, William E. Simon Foundation, and Walton Family Foundation. We appreciate the support of all and are particularly grateful to Peter Flanigan, Roger Hertog, and Bruce Kovner, who took the risk of backing the initial *Ednext* survey. We very much regret the passing of Peter Flanigan as the book neared completion.

We express special thanks to Alan Altshuler and Edward Glazer, directors of the Taubman Center on State and Local Government at the Harvard Kennedy School, which has provided PEPG with essential office space and other key assistance since PEPG's founding in 1996. We are no less appreciative of the continuing support for *Ednext* operations by the Hoover Institution at Stanford University. This volume is sponsored by the Hoover Institution's Koret Task Force on K-12 Education, and we are grateful for comments on earlier drafts by its members, John Chubb, Williamson Evers, Chester Finn Jr., Eric Hanushek, Paul Hill, Caroline Hoxby, Tom Loveless, Terry Moe, Grover Whitehurst, and Herbert Wahlberg.

We appreciate the timely and consistent professional services of Knowledge Networks (KN), an online survey organization that maintains a large, nationally representative sample of households, thereby creating the opportunity to survey special populations and conduct novel experiments. That the KN online survey has been validated as being as reliable as conventional telephone surveys provides solid underpinning for this research.

Matthew Chingos, Terry Moe, Nina Rees, and Jerome Robinson gave numerous helpful suggestions as the surveys were in preparation. Antonio Wendland paid the bills while keeping accounts and procedures in order. Ron Berry, Ashley Inman, Alexandra Mandzak, Maura Roche, and Nick Tavares prepared figures and tables in addition to carrying out a multiplicity of other staff services. We are particularly indebted to William G. Howell, our survey director, who insisted that teachers be surveyed and imaginative experiments be designed. He is an author of many of the articles that foreshadow this publication, including, with Michael Henderson, an essay that was the first to report sharp differences between teacher opinion and public opinion. Howell has been a never-ending source of sensible, insightful commentary, and he always ensured that the *Ednext* survey operated smoothly. Were he not focused on his studies of presidential power, Howell would be a co-author of this volume, not just of chapter 6.

Finally, we offer special thanks to our families, particularly our wives, Carol Peterson, Jeanne Henderson, and Grace West, for their unfailing patience, encouragement, and companionship.

Though we depended on all of these sources of support and guidance, any errors are ours alone.

Paul E. Peterson
Michael Henderson
Martin R. West

CHAPTER ONE

The Education Iron Triangle

WHEN CHICAGO TEACHERS closed the city's schools for seven days in September 2012, their demands went beyond the usual. In addition to asking for a salary increase, the Chicago Teachers Union (CTU) objected to a longer school day, teacher evaluations based on student test scores, merit pay, and the creation of additional charter schools. Two years earlier, Karen Lewis had overthrown—by a 60 percent margin—CTU's reigning leadership. She and a number of other teachers had previously read Naomi Klein's *Shock Doctrine,* a breathless exposé of the privatization of public sector operations in nations across the globe. The group picked Lewis to lead a campaign to persuade Chicago's teachers that CTU's leadership was acquiescing to the same dynamic right before their eyes.

Once elected, Lewis found a new nemesis—the recently elected mayor, Rahm Emmanuel, fresh from his stint in Washington, D.C., as the White House chief of staff to President Barack Obama. "Rahm, being Rahm," one observer said, "wanted to make Chicago the epicenter for reform nationally."[1] During Emmanuel's campaign, he and Lewis had a private dinner of the sort that mayoral candidates like to have with leaders of powerful interest groups. While the conversation seemed to go well enough at the time, their relationship fell apart after Lewis told a reporter that the incoming mayor had said that a quarter of the students in Chicago were "never going to make it and he wasn't going to throw money at the problem." Needless to say, Emmanuel denied the statement, and the experience undoubtedly strengthened his resolve.

Nor did Lewis have much time for another prominent Obama administration official, Secretary of Education Arne Duncan. While superintendent of Chicago's schools, Duncan had opened charter schools and introduced a policy that made it easier for principals to dismiss untenured teachers that they deemed ineffective. In one remarkable incident, Lewis mocked him for an alleged speech impediment: "This guy who has the nerve to stand up and say, 'Education is the thivil rights ithue of our time.' You know he went to private school because if he had gone to public school he'd have had that lisp fixed."[2]

Lewis had little tolerance for "reform unionism," the label that President Randi Weingarten of the American Federation of Teachers (AFT) was seeking to affix to her organization, the more politically astute of the country's two major teacher unions. The other, the National Education Association (NEA), has many more members, but its constituency is disproportionately concentrated in smaller towns and suburban areas. In addition, it has faced frequent turnovers in leadership, making it difficult for a single national spokesperson to emerge. The AFT, by contrast, has an urban constituency with an especially substantial presence in New York state, where the national media also are concentrated. That fact had been exploited by Al Shanker, who, after participating in a series of strikes that won collective bargaining rights for New York City teachers, served as president of the AFT for nearly a quarter-century and became the voice of the organized teaching profession. Although Shanker was criticized for aggressively opposing affirmative action policies in New York City, he gradually won respect for his considered views on everything from national curricular standards to charter schools.

No one was quite able to replace Shanker once he passed from the scene in the closing years of the last century until Randi Weingarten, elected to the same office in 2008, managed to acquire similar stature through her embrace of reform unionism. Reform unionism is based on the idea that teacher unions should collaborate with management in the process of reforming schools, accommodating (and shaping) proposals for change typically deemed anathema to union interests. Weingarten earned accolades by exhibiting an open mind on student testing (if carefully done), charter schools (if properly regulated), and merit pay (if properly designed). In Weingarten's view, teacher unions had to sway with the winds of change, and the reform wind was blowing gustily during the first decade of the twenty-first century. Too much resistance and a strong gale might fell trees that had been nurtured for decades.

CTU leadership had been stout supporters of Weingarten's reform unionism, but Karen Lewis would have none of that. A true citizen of what Carl Sandburg called the City of Broad Shoulders, she wanted to fight back using the union's ultimate weapon, the strike, to stall reform initiatives. After all, Shanker had employed a strike to win collective bargaining rights for New York City teachers in the midst of the 1960 Kennedy-Nixon presidential campaign. His success inspired strikes in Chicago in the early 1970s, through which teachers also won collective bargaining rights, major salary increases, and more favorable working conditions.[3]

After those halcyon days, strikes went out of fashion. Teacher unions discovered that tough but quiet backroom bargaining generally secured the same goals with far less fuss and public risk. But Karen Lewis felt that teachers were steadily losing ground. With the 2002 passage of the federal law, No Child Left Behind Act (NCLB), school reform had gained a certain ascendancy.[4] Regular student testing demonstrated that many students, especially minority students in urban centers, were not meeting state proficiency standards in reading and math. According to the National Assessment of Educational Progress, only 11 percent of African American eighth graders and 15 percent of Hispanic eighth graders were proficient in mathematics.[5] U.S. students as a whole trailed their peers in top-scoring countries abroad by wide margins. A new type of school, the charter school, which typically had a non-union teaching staff, was beginning to compete with the traditional public school. Although charter schools remained few in number, their popularity was growing. Even worse, demands for evaluation of teacher performance, creation of merit pay programs for teachers, and revision of teacher tenure policy had received widespread endorsement, including that of President Obama himself. Newly formed groups such as the Black Alliance for Educational Options (BAEO) and Democrats for Education Reform were broadening the reform coalition beyond its original Republican base.

Rahm Emmanuel epitomized the new risks that unions were facing. A former Democratic congressman from Chicago who had always had solid union backing, Emmanuel nonetheless campaigned for mayor on a school reform platform. He favored merit pay, charter schools, and a longer school day.[6] When elected, he appointed two charter school supporters to his school board and named one of them its president.

For Lewis, the opening of the school year in the middle of the 2012 presidential campaign provided an opportunity not unlike the one that Shanker had enjoyed in 1960. A strike would put teacher power on display for the whole nation to see. From the top of the ticket to the bottom of the ballot, Democratic candidates would not want to risk losing the support of teacher unions, a cornerstone of their electoral coalition. The mayor would be forced to collapse before teacher demands. And the boldness of the strike's timing would send a message to President Obama and Secretary Duncan that the days of tolerance for Democrats who drifted too far from union interests would be numbered. Reform unionism would be sent to its grave.

After a biblical seven days, a compromise was struck, children returned to school, and the debate began over which side had won. Lewis had plenty to crow about. Despite the school system's severe budget crisis, the union had won a salary increase of no less than 16 percent over four years. Also, the teacher evaluation system was designed in such a way as to barely, if at all, comply with a new Illinois law mandating that student test scores be incorporated into teacher ratings. Yet the agreement did not preclude the formation of new charter schools, which were eroding traditional public school enrollments, forcing additional district schools to close, and limiting the number of teachers that the district would need in the future.

Teachers and Reform

As suggested by the ease with which Karen Lewis mobilized her members in Chicago, many rank-and-file teachers do not back reform unionism, to say nothing of the more aggressive agenda promoted by the likes of Mayor Emmanuel. But just how widespread is teacher opposition to rigorous teacher evaluations, school accountability, teacher pension reform, merit pay, charter schools, school vouchers, and other items on the reform agenda? How does teacher opinion compare with that of the general public? Are they essentially in agreement on the most important issues? Or is there a wide gap between the views that teachers hold and those held by parents, taxpayers, and the public as a whole? And how does the stance taken by teachers compare with the positions held by African American and Hispanic citizens, who arguably have the most to gain from improvements to the country's most troubled schools? If quality education is the civil rights issue of our time, as Secretary Duncan has said, then it is worth knowing whether teachers and these minority groups are on the same page.

The Chicago strike confirms that teacher organizations have the clout to shape education policy. The routine participation of these organizations in the collective bargaining process gives teachers a special seat at the policymaking table available to no other group involved in school governance. Furthermore, the collection of union dues directly from teacher paychecks, a common practice in many school districts, augments teacher power by generating resources that can be used in political campaigns for school board, state, and national elections.

But does the disproportionate power of teachers in education policymaking cause problems for democratic governance? If teachers and the public have a common vision, there is no reason to fear teacher influence in the politics of American education. Indeed, if that is the case, the public can safely rely on teacher power to promote common goals. But if the divisions of opinion between teachers and the public are deep, not just in Chicago but throughout the country, then the conflict between Lewis and Emmanuel may have more general import.

For Randi Weingarten, the answers to these questions are obvious: "Parents, the public, and teachers share the same beliefs about the importance of good teaching and strong neighborhood schools. For all who care about kids, the challenge is to act on this shared vision."[7] Karen Lewis is no less insistent that she and her union are fighting for everyone, not just for teachers. "The fight is not about Karen Lewis," she shouted to her cheering followers. "This fight is about the very soul of public education—not only in Chicago but everywhere." In her view, "Our children are not numbers on a spreadsheet: When you come after our children, you come after us."[8]

But union leaders, when issuing public statements, may make claims about public support that are not altogether justified. In the aftermath of the teacher strike, the National Opinion Research Center (NORC), a respected polling firm associated with the University of Chicago, administered a survey to a cross-section of the Chicago public. Nearly two-thirds of respondents favored the expansion of charter schools within the city, while less than one-third opposed the idea. Nearly three-fourths favored merit pay for teachers, and almost the same fraction favored the withdrawal of tenure from teachers found to be consistently ineffective. More than half favored closing some schools in order to help balance the school budget, although 41 percent disagreed with that choice. The NORC poll did not report teacher views on these issues, so one cannot be sure of the extent to which teachers and the public differed on the key issues at the heart of the Chicago strike. But NORC's results do suggest that the similarity of public and teacher opinions is more problematic than either Weingarten's or Lewis's statements assume. That, in any case, is a topic that we intend to explore systematically—with the help of a simple metaphor: the iron triangle.

Iron Triangles

Triangles are the strongest, most rigid, most solid, of basic geometric forms. Circles are slippery, rectangles wobble, and parallelograms collapse at the least provocation. But triangles relentlessly resist change. That's why the three-legged stool is sturdy, the tricycle stable, and the ancient pyramid an architectural triumph.

On Earth, iron is a pervasive element; it forms much of the planet's outer and inner core, and it is one of the most common elements found on Earth's crust. When iron is smelted, impurities harden and strengthen it. When first used for agricultural purposes and armed conflict, iron transformed economic relationships, cultures, and belief systems. When iron is cast as a triangular form, the object is tough, strong, and powerful. For political analysts, the iron triangle is the perfect metaphor for characterizing one of the strongest, most stable, and most pervasive aspects of American politics—the connection among producer interests, elected officials, and actions taken by government agencies.

Metaphorically speaking, representatives of producer and occupation-based interest groups—oil barons, banks, auto companies, trial lawyers, farmers, and the like—constitute the base of an isosceles triangle. They serve hard, highly concentrated, powerful interests. Those interests connect and support the triangle's other two sides. By means of steady communication and financial contributions, representatives of producer

Figure 1-1. *The Education Iron Triangle*

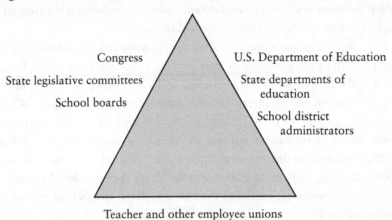

Congress
State legislative committees
School boards

U.S. Department of Education
State departments of education
School district administrators

Teacher and other employee unions
Vendors

groups build close relationships with the senators and representatives who serve on relevant committees in Congress, state legislators who act in the same capacity at the middle tier of government, and local officials who serve on special boards and commissions that affect the well-being of the producer group. The third side of the triangle is formed by the government agencies that produce goods, regulations, and services of interest to the producer group (figure 1-1).

On a two-dimensional plane, an iron triangle encloses a space that is virtually impossible to penetrate. As a metaphor, it captures the reality that producer groups excel at discovering channels of communication that access information unavailable to the general public. Iron triangle politics are quiet, operating beneath the radar, almost in secret. To capture special benefits from the public trough, the producer group needs to belly up to the goodies while squeezing others to the side.

Producer groups succeed in insulating policy decisions from external pressures because they have the focus and resources to pursue their goals effectively; the attention of the general public, in contrast, is too episodic and scattered to have an impact, except in times of crisis. In the midst of a financial meltdown, banks may find their privileges crimped by a suddenly aroused Congress. If gas prices and profit margins soar in tandem,

tax loopholes benefiting the oil industry may be closed. But times of crisis are the exception, iron triangle theory tells us. Ordinarily, the iron triangle operates quietly—at the public's expense.

For the iron triangle metaphor to apply, however, the interests and
desires of the producer groups that form the triangle must differ from
those of the general public. If the public and the producer group agree, it
makes no difference whether decisions are made by iron triangles. What
the special groups insist on, the public wants as well. In this heavenly
world, the iron triangle is nothing but a trio of angels. On the planet
Earth, however, producer group interests are seldom so benign. If not
quite nefarious, they are at least discordant with the considered views of
citizens and consumers excluded from the insulated spaces that producer
groups fabricate.

School Politics, Conventionally Understood

Curiously, the iron triangle metaphor is seldom applied to school politics.[9]
The politics of education is typically presented as either an extension of

—the culture wars: Should schools teach evolution? Should they sup-
ply teenagers with condoms?

—class conflict: Do the affluent stand in the way of efforts to equalize
school spending?

—generational differences: Will the elderly pay for the schools of the
next generation?

—just another issue that divides Democrats from Republicans along
familiar lines: Are schools a state and local responsibility, or is there a role
for the federal government?

or, most persuasively,

—a crucial component of the ongoing racial and ethnic divide: Is more
desegregation needed? Are African American and Hispanic students
receiving a quality education?

Although the iron triangle metaphor has been invoked in condemna-
tions of teacher unions, such criticism has often focused on the misguided
actions of union bosses rather than on the views of the teachers that the
unions claim to represent.

Teachers themselves are thought to be just like us—or, more exactly,
just like our better selves. Admittedly, the schoolmaster of the colonial

period did not enjoy such a lofty perch in the American mythology. In a best-selling book, John Locke warned families against schooling their children for fear of contaminating their morals. In the short story "The Legend of Sleepy Hollow," published in 1820, author Washington Irving arranged for the ungainly teacher Ichabod Crane to be hounded out of a Hudson Valley town. A few decades later, Americans cried with their British cousins over the beatings that headmaster Mr. Creakle administered to David Copperfield. But even as Dickens was writing, a rapidly expanding public education system, staffed by young, unmarried women with talents that far exceeded their level of compensation, altered the American schoolteacher's public image.

In the twentieth century, the teacher became an admired figure in American popular culture. It was not only Mr. Chips (Robert Donat), the ill-starred educator in the 1939 British film classic, who captured American hearts. The selfless public servant Richard Dadier (Glenn Ford) subdued the *Blackboard Jungle* in 1955. Twelve years later, rookie teacher Sylvia Barrett (Sandy Denis) offered her compassion and dedication to troubled students in an overcrowded New York City high school in *Up the Down Staircase*, while Mark Thackeray (Sidney Poitier) won the affection and respect of a classroom of rebellious students in London's East End in *To Sir, with Love*. The year 1988 saw Jaime Escalante (Edward James Olmos) *Stand and Deliver* instruction that inspired his East Los Angeles students to succeed in advanced placement calculus. Seven years later, Mr. Holland (Richard Dreyfus) showed that teaching has the power to change lives in *Mr. Holland's Opus*, while LouAnne Johnson (Michelle Pfeiffer) stood by her inner-city students when no one else would in *Dangerous Minds*. In 2007, Erin Gruwell (Hillary Swank) reached her freshmen English students at a racially and ethnically divided California high school in *Freedom Writers*.

It is not only in the movies that educators are beloved. Unlike lawyers, bankers, used-car dealers, and state legislators, teachers maintain a superb reputation. Most of us remember at least one teacher who had a decisively positive impact on our lives. We see them as selfless members of a helping profession. Most Americans say that teachers have "very great prestige," an accolade otherwise given by a majority of the public only to firefighters, scientists, doctors, nurses, and military officers. Other occupations pale by comparison. Just 11 percent, for example, give stolid, sensible accountants that same rating.[10]

Perhaps for that reason, the public has held fast to governing arrangements that isolate education from the mainstream of political life. American school districts operate as single-purpose governments, typically with their own taxing authority. They are governed by school boards chosen through nonpartisan elections often held on days other than the first Tuesday after the first Monday in November, when national elections are held. Because schools are for children, Progressive-era reformers saw fit to remove them from the dirtier aspects of partisan conflict. And special deference was given to the professional administrators whose expertise was thought to be needed to make schools function effectively.

While that quiet serenity marked much school decisionmaking in the golden years immediately following World War II, the situation changed dramatically in the closing decades of the twentieth century as a result of fractious legal disputes, teacher strikes, and collective bargaining agreements. In recent years, governors, mayors, and even school boards have regularly come into conflict with the organized representatives of the teaching profession. Wisconsin's new limitations on teachers' collective bargaining rights provoked major protests in early 2011. Debates over union rights and prerogatives have since percolated in states as politically diverse as Indiana, Florida, Ohio, Illinois, Massachusetts, and California. Meanwhile, in school districts from Washington, D.C., to Los Angeles and Seattle, teacher unions and superintendents have clashed over the use of new evaluation systems that base compensation on student test scores. And as we have seen, reform efforts provoked a bitter teacher strike in Chicago.

Yet few analysts have identified an iron triangle at the heart of education politics and policymaking. That oversight is understandable given the centrality of the race issue to American public education in the wake of the 1954 Supreme Court decision *Brown* v. *Board of Education*. School desegregation provoked racial conflict in Birmingham, Montgomery, Chicago, Boston, Los Angeles, Detroit, New York City, and other cities across the country, often for years at a time. Even after things settled down, a sharp racial division was carved between the predominantly minority schools in central cities and the overwhelmingly white schools in suburban areas. For generations, eyes have been focused on disparities in the achievement levels and graduation rates of white and minority students. For much of the latter half of the twentieth century, the politics of American education was rightly interpreted in racial terms. Leading scholarly books devoted to school politics bore such titles as *The Color of School Reform*, *"Brown" in Baltimore*, *The Education Gap*, and *The Shame of the Nation: The Restoration of Apartheid Schooling in America.*[11]

Today, that characterization captures only one part of the education story. In the twenty-first century, school integration, while certainly desirable, no longer seems sufficient. Too many black students, even those in predominantly white schools, continue to trail their white peers; too many schools have remained segregated for too long; too little attention is being given to teaching students how to read, write, and calculate. The debate over school integration now requires discussion of school accountability, parental choice, and measures designed to enhance the quality of the teacher workforce. The focus of education reform discussions has shifted from the question of which school a child should attend to the learning that takes place within a school. On these newer issues, the views of those inside and outside the iron triangle might be quite different.

Public Opinion and Teacher Opinion

This shift in the policy discussion provides the context for our analysis. In the chapters that follow, we identify the extent of the disagreement between groups within the general public on a wide range of school-related issues. We give special attention to the size of differences of opinion between teachers and the public at large. Does the public in fact favor changes in public education that members of the teaching profession reject? Is the dominant political cleavage with respect to education policy between an organized producer group and the general public? Or are other social and political divisions, especially those affecting race and ethnic relations, of greater significance? In the conclusion, we explore the potential interaction between the strains generated by the divide between those inside and outside the iron triangle and those fostered by the continuing racial divide on many school policies.

Under the auspices of the Harvard Program on Education Policy and Governance and the journal *Education Next*, we have gathered information designed to answer these questions through seven annual surveys of nationally representative samples of the U.S. adult population, conducted between 2007 and 2013 (hereafter referred to as the *EdNext* polls). In several of those years, we posed the same questions to a nationally representative sample of public school teachers. In 2011 we administered the survey to a larger number of respondents, allowing us to estimate opinion quite precisely for a variety of specialized populations including parents, African Americans, Hispanics, and the more affluent. We also split our sample into two randomly selected halves, posing questions about school policy in the national context to some respondents and the same questions in the context of their local school district or local community to other respondents. In other years, we conducted other survey experiments, asking about the same topic in two different ways to find out how sensitive public opinion was to the specific wording of a question or the specific information made available to the respondent.[12] In chapter 6 we report the results from a survey experiment conducted in 2013 that looks at how information on local district rankings statewide and nationwide affects public opinion. Otherwise, most results reported in this volume come from the 2011 survey; when findings come from other years, we report the year of the survey in the text or accompanying note. Appendixes A through C provide details on survey design, the exact wording of questions, and the full distribution of responses to questions from the 2011 survey.[13]

Plan of the Book

In chapter 2, we show that teacher opinion differs from that of the general public on many, though not all, education policies. In chapter 3 we show that the overall cleavage between teachers and the general public is wider than other divisions, such as those between parents of school-age children and other adults, between young and old respondents, and between Democrats and Republicans. Other large divides are seen between whites and African Americans and whites and Hispanics. Still, much of school politics is rooted in a conflict between producers within the triangular space and the public outside it.

In chapter 4, we show that the teacher-public divide is not confined to issues presented in the national context. Even when a question is framed in terms of the respondent's own school district or community, the teacher-public divide remains apparent. In chapter 5, we report that the public is not well-informed about key aspects of education policy, putting at risk its capacity to protect its interests from the power of the education iron triangle. A series of experiments presented in chapters 5 and 6 reveals the extent to which public and teacher opinion shifts when more information is directly provided. Generally speaking, when the public is better informed, the divide between teachers and the public widens.

Chapter 7 looks within the teaching profession. What kinds of individuals become teachers? What kinds of teachers do not agree with the majority? Is the teaching profession changing as younger teachers replace older ones? Although genuine divisions exist within the teaching profession, we conclude that it is unlikely teachers' differences with the general public will erode with the passage of time or that they are well enough defined to threaten the iron triangle. In our concluding chapter, we consider a series of objections to the thesis that we have advanced and examine ways in which racial and ethnic divides could alter the future of the education iron triangle.

CHAPTER TWO

The Teacher-Public Divide

TEACHER POLICY, PARENTAL choice, school accountability, taxes, and spending: all that and more have been tossed into the crucible that forges the politics of American education. The questions under debate are nearly endless: How much should be spent on education? How should teachers be paid? Should students and schools be held accountable? Should teachers have tenure to protect them from losing their jobs? Should families have government assistance that helps them pay the cost of attending private schools? Should more charter schools be allowed to open?

Our surveys do not cover every conceivable topic, but they cut a broad swath. Although we could not inquire about every issue under public discussion, we do ask about twenty-three key topics that collectively shed light on the range and depth of the divide between teachers and the public. We begin this chapter with one of the most salient topics—the recruitment, retention, and compensation of the education workforce. Admittedly, any differences between teachers and the broader public are apt to be largest in this area, which has direct implications for teachers' work lives. At the same time, intense public interest in measures to improve teacher effectiveness has placed these issues at the very top of the contemporary policy agenda.

Teacher Recruitment, Tenure, and Compensation Policies

Teachers vary widely in their effectiveness in raising student achievement. A student with a highly effective rather than an average teacher will have a better chance of going to college and will receive a higher salary when he or she enters the work force.[1] Given the critical role that teachers play, their recruitment, retention, and compensation are crucial to students' educational success. Accordingly, teacher employment policies have come under increasing scrutiny. To be hired, teachers are expected to have a state license, which is most commonly obtained by taking appropriate courses from a school of education. Salary differences are based almost exclusively on the number of years that a teacher has worked for the district and whether he or she has a master's or other advanced degree. As a result, teachers in the same school district are compensated at the same level regardless of their effectiveness. Teacher pensions disproportionately reward those with a long tenure within the state or district retirement system at the expense of new and mobile teachers. Collective bargaining agreements provide extensive protections against dismissal for ineffective teaching. Only a tiny fraction—well under 1 percent—of the tenured teaching force is ever dismissed.[2]

School reform advocates are critical of every one of those policies. In 2009, as superintendent of schools in Washington, D.C., Michelle Rhee put in place a merit pay program and used her authority to remove teachers from classrooms where student performance was below par. Kate Walsh of the National Council on Teacher Quality (NCTQ) says there is little evidence that state-licensed teachers are any better, on average, than those teaching without certification. Nor does she think that a master's degree adds much, if anything, to teacher effectiveness. On the grounds that additional years of teaching beyond the first five are only weakly related to teacher effectiveness, reformers also cast doubt on the wisdom of compensation strategies that reward senior teachers with higher pay and valuable pension benefits. They argue that job protections for ineffective teachers place the interests of teachers ahead of those of students. Walsh would have Congress require every state to set a "minimum percentage" of probationary teachers that school districts "must identify" as low-performing each year, making them eligible for dismissal if their performance does not improve.[3] Jeb Bush, who founded the Foundation for Excellence in Education (Excel in Ed) after completing two terms as Florida governor, has called for an end to teacher tenure and the abandonment of traditional salary schedules in favor of pay-for-performance programs.

By contrast, teacher unions oppose merit pay, tenure limitations, and looser teacher certification requirements. In Chicago, teachers struck in opposition to board proposals to introduce performance evaluations and eliminate the "last-hired, first-fired" rule, which gave preference to senior teachers regardless of their effectiveness. The strike was prolonged into a second school week when negotiators could not agree on "a teacher-evaluation system and a demand that laid-off teachers be the first ones rehired."[4] Explaining her reasons for the strike, union leader Karen Lewis declared, "We want job security."[5]

But what does the public think? Does it agree with school reformers who call for changes in teacher recruitment, retention, and compensation policies, or does it oppose such calls for reform? And how about teachers themselves? Do unions faithfully represent their members' views?

To answer those questions, we compare the opinions of the segment of the teaching force and the public at large that express definite opinions on the issues, ignoring the (at times substantial) segment of the population that do not take a stand one way or the other. Our method for discerning the extent of disagreement between teachers and the general public is best described by discussing in detail our question about merit pay. Specifically, we inquired as to whether teacher salaries should be based, "in part, on their students' progress on state tests." Respondents are asked to choose from the following five options: *Completely favor, Somewhat favor, Neither favor nor oppose, Somewhat oppose,* or *Completely oppose.* As it turns out, 48 percent of the general public favor the idea either somewhat or completely; 26 percent are either somewhat or completely opposed; and roughly one-quarter remain neutral on the issue. Conversely, 76 percent of teachers report that they oppose merit pay either somewhat or completely. Only 14 percent register support, and 9 percent opt not to take a position on the issue (see table 2-1).[6]

We convert the answers to this question into a summary measure of the extent of disagreement between teachers and nonteachers as follows: First we set aside the 9 percent of teachers and the one-quarter of the public who do not take a stand one way or the other. Of the remainder, just 16 percent of teachers express support for merit pay. That contrasts with 66 percent of the public as a whole, suggesting a difference of 50 percentage points between teachers and the public at large in their support for merit pay.

We calculate the differences between teachers and the rest of the public across most of the other issues in the same way. To measure the size of the divide between any two groups on each issue, we calculate the

Table 2-1. *Distribution of General Public and Teacher Opinion on Merit Pay, 2011*[a]

Percent

Issue/opinion	General public	Teachers
Merit pay		
Completely favor	14	5
Somewhat favor	34	9
Neither favor nor oppose	26	9
Somewhat oppose	18	23
Completely oppose	8	53

a. The survey question was "Do you favor or oppose basing the salaries of teachers *around the nation*, in part, on their students' academic progress on state tests?" "Teachers" includes only K–12 public school teachers; "general public" excludes public school teachers.

share in each group that expresses either some or complete support for a policy of all those who take a side (that is, setting aside those who indicated that they neither favor nor oppose) and then calculate the difference between those shares.[7] Readers should keep in mind our analytical strategy when they read that we find a "majority" favoring or opposing a particular policy proposal: the majority is only of those taking a side, not of all respondents.[8]

This metric allows us to summarize the size of the cleavage between public school teachers and the rest of the general public across twenty-three education policies (table 2-2). Entries in bold indicate that majorities of those expressing an opinion take opposing sides on the issue. As it turns out, merit pay, with a differential of 50 percentage points, is the most divisive issue between teachers and the public at large.

Teachers and the public disagree over other teacher employment policies as well. Seventy-six percent of the public think that teachers should demonstrate success in raising student achievement before receiving tenure but only 29 percent of teachers share that view. The total elimination of tenure is supported by 72 percent of the public but by only 35 percent of teachers. Teachers are also more skeptical than the public of allowing principals to hire uncertified applicants and more likely to see teacher unions as having a positive effect on local schools. Indeed, on each of these teacher policy issues, a majority of teachers oppose the position taken by a majority of the public.

Table 2-2. *Opinion Differences between the General Public and Teachers, 2011*[a]

Percent

Issue/opinion	General public	Teachers	Difference between public and teachers
Teacher policy			
Use merit pay	66	16	**−50***
Use merit tenure	76	29	**−46***
Allow flexible hiring	58	30	**−28***
Eliminate tenure	72	35	**−37***
Teacher unions are harmful	57	32	**−25***
School choice			
Expand choice with universal vouchers	65	38	**−27***
Use government funds for means-tested vouchers	51	27	**−24***
Allow charter schools	71	54	−17*
Allow tax credit–funded scholarships	71	51	**−20***
Allow online courses	65	56	−9
Accountability			
Require annual testing	89	65	−24*
Use common standards/test	72	60	−12*
Use test for grade promotion	86	72	−15*
Require graduation test	86	77	−10*
Taxes and spending			
Increase spending	64	71	6
Raise taxes	35	49	**14***
Raise teacher pay	54	80	26*
Increase teacher share of benefit costs	66	29	**−37***
Cultural issues			
Allow single-sex schools	59	71	12*
Grant principal final disciplinary authority	40	57	**17***
Allow time for silent prayer	69	58	−11*
Diversity			
Use family income to assign students	37	37	0
Separate classes for disturbed students	65	67	2

a. Boldface type indicates that among those with an opinion on the question, a majority of teachers and a majority of the public were on opposite sides. See appendix B for the wording of the questions. Questions are the national, not the local, wording option given in the appendix. Questions on principal's authority and school prayer were posed in 2008. Differences are rounded to the nearest whole number.

* Statistically significant at the 0.05 level.

When it comes to setting the terms for teacher employment, public policy today is more consistent with teacher opinion than with that of the public as a whole. While merit pay plans were enacted during Rhee's tenure in Washington, D.C., and have been introduced in other locales, only a few districts around the country have significantly modified traditional practices, which compensate teachers according to experience and credentials without regard to performance.[9] Only a few districts have eased the process by which teachers can be dismissed if they are shown to be ineffective, and traditional teacher certification policies remain largely intact in most states, though in some states teachers can begin teaching before obtaining certification. On these issues, policy seems more responsive to those inside the iron triangle than to the public at large.

School Choice

In 1955 Milton Friedman proposed a dramatic restructuring of the country's education system: every family should choose its child's school, whether public or private, religious or secular, with the government covering the cost.[10] In his view, students and families would identify the schools that they prefer, and schools would adapt until their offerings matched consumer demand. Continuous competition among schools would generate continuous improvement in education.

In the more than half-century since Friedman wrote his essay, a multiplicity of school choice proposals have been advanced in local school districts, state legislatures, and the halls of Congress. School voucher programs for children from low-income families who wish to attend private schools have been established in Milwaukee, Wisconsin; Cleveland, Ohio; Washington, D.C.; the state of Indiana; and elsewhere. Tax credits for business or individual contributions to foundations that provide scholarships to low-income families for private school tuition are available in Pennsylvania, Florida, Arizona, New Hampshire, and other states. Charter schools, privately managed schools authorized by a government entity, have been created in more than forty states. And in a few states—Florida, Utah, and Idaho—high school students can take some of their courses online while obtaining the remainder at their local district high school. The expansion of school choice remains central to such diverse school reform organizations as the Black Alliance for Educational Options; StudentsFirst, led by Michelle

Rhee; Excel in Ed, led by Jeb Bush; and the Friedman Foundation for Educational Choice.

Teacher unions oppose nearly all school choice proposals. Hostility to voucher and tax credit plans is intense, and unions have grown increasingly critical of charter schools. The National Education Association (NEA) does not formally oppose charter schools as long as they conform to a lengthy set of conditions and do not adversely affect the funding of traditional public schools, but it does say that "charter school employees should have the same collective bargaining rights—under both state law and local practice—as their counterparts in mainstream public schools."[11] In practice, local teacher unions typically oppose charter expansion. Indeed, it was the growing presence of charter schools in Chicago that energized the group that Karen Lewis brought to power. A member of Lewis's coterie explained its thinking in these terms: "We increasingly had this sense that if we didn't do something, you could wind the film forward ten years and there wasn't going to be much left of our public school system or our union."[12] When the Chicago school board announced plans to close some public schools, Karen Lewis fought the move, complaining that "the attack on public schools is endemic" and claiming that the closures were designed to open the doors to new charter schools.[13] Diane Ravitch, a New York University professor with close ties to union leaders, puts the case against charter schools in especially stark terms: "The continued growth of charter schools in urban districts will leave regular public schools with the most difficult students to educate," she says, "thus creating a two-tier system of widening inequality. . . . The regular public schools in the nation's cities will be locked into a downward trajectory . . . an ominous development . . . for our nation."[14] Her conclusion: "Our schools cannot improve if charter schools siphon away the most motivated students and their families . . . from the regular public schools."[15]

Although school choice programs have begun to spread, only in a select few settings, such as New Orleans and the District of Columbia, have they established themselves as a major alternative to the traditional public school. The most popular school choice option, the charter school, serves fewer than 5 percent of public school students nationwide. Is that small percentage due to opposition to choice from within the education iron triangle? Or does the public agree with the critics of school choice? To find out, we pose five questions that inquire about support for

—voucher programs to expand choice for all students

—voucher programs for low-income students

—tax credits to fund private school scholarships

—formation of charter schools

—awarding students credit for courses taken online.

Majorities of the public favor all five school choice options. Over 70 percent favor tax credits and charter schools; 65 percent back online learning and school vouchers for all students; and 51 percent support targeted voucher programs serving low-income students.

Teacher opinion diverges sharply from that of the general public on all of these issues except for online learning. With that exception, the differences between teachers and the public range from 17 to 24 percentage points. Judging by the gap between the amount of school choice available to parents and the state of public opinion, education triangle opposition is a likely explanation for the spotty, limited nature of the school choice movement's successes.

In contrast to the wide disparities between the views of teachers and those of the public on most forms of school choice, their differences with respect to online learning are narrow. That may reflect different understandings of the meaning of online learning, an innovation still in its infancy. Some think of online learning as taking place within regular classrooms while others think of it as an alternative, more akin to homeschooling, whereby the student communicates with a teacher only over the Internet or by telephone. It remains to be seen whether teachers and the public will continue to support online learning in nearly equal measure if its use outside regular classrooms spreads.

School Accountability

School accountability has until recently been a less controversial issue than either school choice or merit pay. When No Child Left Behind (NCLB) was enacted into law in 2002, it required states to ask districts to report publicly annual student performance on state tests administered in grades three through eight and given once in high school. At the time, unions did not play a major public role in the accountability discussions. Behind the scenes, unions did not oppose standards, testing, or the release of information on school performance, but they did not want the government to impose strong penalties—financial or otherwise—on schools that did not live up to expectations. They took a similar stance with respect to state accountability legislation passed in the years leading up to NCLB's passage.[16] NCLB required the release of test results at the school level, but it did not mandate test-based consequences for students. However, Florida and Chicago initiated a requirement that students pass tests to advance from one grade to the next at key points in their educational careers, and many other states required students to pass a test in order to graduate from high school. Teacher unions have often acquiesced—and sometimes have supported—the passage of such legislation. Albert Shanker once defined school reform as policies that included "rigorous academic standards, assessments based on those standards, incentives for students to work hard in school and genuine professional accountability."[17]

Though union opposition to the accountability provisions in NCLB was tepid at the time of enactment, it increased steadily as the law was being implemented. Eventually, the NEA filed lawsuits aimed at forestalling its implementation. Teacher union opposition hardened when information on student performance gathered in compliance with NCLB requirements was used to ascertain teacher effectiveness, and some states and school districts, with the encouragement of the Obama administration, considered using the information to institute performance pay. This issue was central to the Chicago strike. Union president Karen Lewis stated her position in these words:

> Too much of the new evaluations will be based on students' standardized test scores. This is no way to measure the effectiveness of an educator. Further, there are too many factors beyond our control which impact how well some students perform on standardized tests, such as poverty, exposure to violence, homelessness, hunger and other social issues beyond our control.[18]

In the wake of the Chicago strike, the anti-testing movement spread. In Seattle, teachers went on strike rather than administer standardized tests to ninth-graders. Diane Ravitch, too, denounces testing and accountability policies:

NCLB was a punitive law based on erroneous assumptions about how to improve schools. It assumed that reporting test scores to the public would be an effective lever for school reform. It assumed that changes in governance would lead to school improvement. It assumed that shaming schools that were unable to lift test scores every year—and the people who work in them—would lead to higher scores. It assumed that low scores are caused by lazy teachers and lazy principals, who need to be threatened with the loss of their jobs. . . . Testing is not a substitute for curriculum and instruction. Good education cannot be achieved by a strategy of testing children, shaming educators and closing schools.[19]

To get a sense of public and teacher opinion about accountability, we asked:

—whether the federal government should continue to mandate that all students be tested annually in grades 3–8

—whether states should adopt common standards and tests

—whether state tests should be used to decide whether a student is promoted to the next grade

—whether students should have to demonstrate proficiency on state tests in order to graduate from high school.

The answers to these questions were markedly one-sided. On few issues does the American public speak with one voice, but accountability in public education comes close to fitting that bill. Over 85 percent of the public favor maintaining NCLB's core testing requirements; testing students for promotion from one grade to the next; and requiring students to pass an examination in order to graduate from high school. And over 70 percent think that common national standards and examinations should be established and adopted across all states.[20] No wonder accountability laws abound and the current drive toward establishing common standards in core subjects nationwide has drawn support from both Republican and Democratic elected officials.

A clear majority of teachers who choose a side on this issue also favor accountability. Over 70 percent favor both examinations for promotion from one grade to the next and for high school graduation, and over 60 percent favor continuation of federal testing and the establishment of national standards. Although those percentages are lower than the overwhelming levels of support expressed by the public at large, accountability politics has been shaped less by education triangle opposition than has teacher policy and school choice politics. At this point there is no clear sign that the teaching force has been persuaded that accountability measures are wrong-headed.

That could change, of course, if student tests come to be used as a basis for making teacher compensation and tenure decisions. In 2012 we asked teachers how much weight should be given in teacher evaluations to the test performance of their students and how much to the principal's assessment. Their reply: 27 percent of the weight should be given to tests and 74 percent to the principal's judgment. The public, in contrast, assigns 54 percent of the weight to tests and 46 percent to the principal's assessment. If school accountability segues into teacher accountability, the teacher-public divide can be expected to widen considerably.

School Finance and Teacher Salaries

At first glance, school spending seems to be an issue on which teachers and the public see eye to eye. When asked about spending in their local school district, a majority of both groups report that it should increase rather than stay about the same or decrease. Yet when asked about raising "taxes to fund public schools," roughly half of teachers but just 35 percent of the general public say that taxes should increase. Not surprisingly, teachers are also far more enthusiastic than the public at large about increasing teacher salaries: as much as 80 percent of teachers but only 54 percent of the public support salary increases.

Teachers and the public are also divided over financing school employee benefits. When asked whether teachers should be required to pay 20 percent of the cost of health care and pension benefits, with the government covering the rest, two-thirds of the public support such a requirement but only 29 percent of teachers do.

The teacher-public gap widens further when both are provided with basic facts about actual spending levels and salary levels. As we show in chapter 5, teachers and the public differ over school finance and teacher salaries nearly as much as they do on teacher employment policy questions when information on current expenditures and salaries is made available.

Cultural Issues

We do not inquire into the full range of cultural issues that have sprung to the fore at local school board meetings and in state referenda. We do not pose questions about hotly contested curricular issues such as how to approach the topics of sex education or evolution or the appropriateness of corporal punishment in schools. But we have inquired about three widely debated topics: single-sex schools, prayer in public school, and whether principals should have the final say on school suspensions.

Generally, school reform groups have not waded into controversies over cultural and social issues. Although Democrats for Education Reform has endorsed legal recognition of same-sex marriage, silence is more common among groups like the Black Alliance for Educational Options, Students First, Excel in Ed, and the National Council on Teacher Quality. For the unions, too, cultural issues are generally not a priority, although the NEA has taken a liberal stance on some. For example, it questioned the legality of regulations promulgated by the Bush administration in 2004 that gave institutions the right to establish single-sex schools and single-sex classrooms.[21] In 2012 it also promoted a national moratorium on school suspensions, arguing that they aggravated educational disparities. And it opposes prayer and other religious practices in school.[22]

Despite the positions taken by the NEA, the split between teachers and the public on cultural matters is marginal and inconsistent from one topic to the next. Consider, for example, the issue of the legal protection that students should have before being suspended. In 1975 the Supreme Court ruled that suspending a student for ten days without a hearing and right of counsel violated the student's right to due process. Since that decision, many school districts have developed elaborate procedures that require hearings and school board action before students can be suspended or expelled from school. Critics have argued that such complex procedures undermine the authority of teachers and principals.[23] In 2008 we asked the public for an opinion on this issue in the following way:

> Some people say that principals should be the final authority on disciplinary matters. Other people say that students who have been suspended from school have a right to appeal their punishment to the local school board. Which do you think is preferable?

Only 40 percent of the public think that principals should be "the final authority," but 57 percent of teachers do. That teachers take the more conservative stance is not surprising, as they may feel that detailed due process procedures complicate their exercise of effective classroom discipline.

It is perhaps more surprising to learn that teachers are also more likely to favor giving parents the option of choosing a single-sex school. In 2008, 65 percent of teachers but only 60 percent of the public were so inclined. Three years later, 71 percent of teachers but only 59 percent of the general public expressed a willingness to allow single-sex education. Even more interesting is the fact that teachers were somewhat more likely to say that they would consider sending their own child to a single-sex school (48 percent) than was the public as a whole (42 percent).

The one issue on which teachers take a more liberal stance involved school prayer. Since open prayer in school has been declared unconstitutional, we inquired whether the public thought that "time in each day [should] be set aside for silent prayer and reflection." While only 58 percent of teachers respond favorably to that question, 69 percent of the general public do. Nonetheless, large majorities of both the public and teachers embrace a stance more conservative than that implied by the NEA's position on school prayer.

If the responses that we receive are representative of the broader cultural divisions within the United States, there is no reason to think that views on these kinds of issues at the grassroots level of the teaching profession are dramatically more liberal than those of the general public. The key issues on which teachers part ways with the public are those affecting their jobs—salaries, tenure, and school choice—matters that for teachers, and also for most education reform groups, are separate from broader cultural conflicts.

Diversity

In 2007, the Supreme Court decided that explicit assignment of students to schools for the purpose of promoting racial integration violates the Equal Protection Clause of the Fourteenth Amendment. But many school districts have continued similar practices, and others have introduced family income as an alternative assignment criterion for encouraging social diversity within schools and classrooms. On this issue, too, both school reformers and teacher unions are more apt to remain silent than to take a strong position one way or another. Still, NEA has lauded within-school diversity. As its president, Dennis Van Rockel, put it, "NEA has a long and proud history of supporting affirmative action. . . . We know without a doubt that diverse classrooms better prepare students for a diverse work-force and life in our vibrant, diverse society."[24]

To see whether teachers and the public are more supportive of an affirmative action policy based on student income than one based on race, we divided respondents to our 2008 survey into random halves. To the first group, we asked the following affirmative action question: "In order to promote school diversity, should public school districts be allowed to take the racial background of students into account when assigning students to schools?" Only 21 percent of the general public like the idea. Surprisingly, given the NEA position, support among teachers is not much higher—only 24 percent favor race-based affirmative action. The second group was asked the same question except that we substituted the words "family income" for the words "racial background." Only 17 percent of the public and 22 percent of the teachers are favorably disposed to income-based assignment. Opposition to income-based affirmative action is as great as opposition to race-based affirmative action.

Three years later, in 2011, we once again inquired about income-based affirmative action but framed our question in a manner that was much friendlier to the idea. We dropped references to school diversity, substituting instead the positive language "ensure a mix of students." Specifically, we asked: "Should school districts across the country take the family income into account when assigning students to schools in order to ensure that each school has a mix of students from different backgrounds?" When the question was worded in that way, both public and teacher support shifted upward, to 37 percent. Nonetheless, clear majorities of both teachers and the public express a lack of enthusiasm for the idea. Affirmative action policy does not divide those inside and outside the iron triangle.

The practice of mainstreaming students with emotional or behavioral disabilities by placing them in regular classrooms during much of the school day has spread quickly, but it has not become a major public issue.[25] The percentage of students diagnosed with an emotional disturbance who spend more than 80 percent of their time in a regular classroom jumped from 17 percent to 35 percent during the decade ending in

2005. In Scranton, Pennsylvania, the issue provoked enough resistance from teachers that it became a collective bargaining issue. The president of the local parents' group was no less concerned: "The general consensus is that it doesn't work having all these kids together."[26] Groups representing the rights of students with disabilities argue that mainstreaming is necessary to integrate marginal students into their peer community, but it is probably not surprising to learn that, when polled, neither teachers nor the public express much support for including students diagnosed with an emotional disturbance in regular classrooms. On this issue, too, teachers and the public think pretty much alike.

Adjustments for Background Characteristics

Table 2-2 reports the differences between teachers and the public on the various issues under consideration. But do teachers hold their positions because they are teachers or because of some other background characteristic that distinguishes them from the general public? After all, teachers are better educated, are more likely to be female, are more likely to be white, have higher incomes, think more highly of their local schools, and are different in other respects as well. Perhaps it is these background characteristics, not the fact of being a teacher, that explain the differences between teachers and the public.

In additional analyses not presented in tabular form, we explore whether demographic differences could account for the cleavage between teachers and the rest of the public on school reform proposals.[27] On all but one issue—income integration of schools—significant differences between teacher and non-teacher opinions remain even after we adjust for the above-mentioned variables. For ten of the items, the size of the teacher coefficient is still very large.[28] Most of the differences between the teaching force and the public are not attributable to the specific composition of the teaching force. Rather, they appear to be driven by the distinctive occupational interests of those who have chosen teaching as a profession.

Specifically, the divergence of opinion between teachers and the general public is both statistically significant and large on teacher policies, school choice, school accountability, and school expenditures. The differences are serious and substantial enough to constitute a political iron triangle. Teachers are, of course, drawn from a broad segment of the public, live and work in every community in the country, and have long been held in high regard by the public as a whole. On social and cultural issues, their views closely resemble those of the public at large; on some matters, teachers' views are more conservative than those expressed by the unions that represent their occupational interests. Still, teachers have occupational interests that they seek to protect—higher pay, a guaranteed job, autonomy without account-ability, and industry protection from competing institutions.

But is the teacher-public cleavage larger than other social and political divides over school policy? After all, parents' interests differ from the interests of those who do not have students in the schools, the interests of the well-to-do are distinct from those of the poor, and various ethnic and cultural groups differ on many policy questions. And Democratic and Republican elected officials spar regularly over issues of school spending and school choice, suggesting that their supporters in the electorate may be similarly divided. Perhaps the teacher-public cleavage pales in com-parison to other social and political divisions. To that topic, we now turn.

CHAPTER THREE

Other Social Divisions

THE GAP BETWEEN the thinking of teachers and the public as a whole may be wide, but other opinion gaps compete for the attention of policy analysts and political leaders. For some, education politics is first and foremost an extension of the culture wars.[1] For others, it is a by-product of class politics, with well-heeled suburbanites resisting measures to use their tax dollars to equalize spending across school district lines.[2] Often, education conflict is cast in generational terms: will senior citizens support adequate education funding even though they have no school-age children, or do they want government funding to be concentrated on services for the elderly?[3] Homeownership is sometimes regarded as the central issue, partly because schools have traditionally been funded by the local property tax.[4] Partisan polarization is a favorite theme whenever education policy is under consideration at the state and the national level. Republicans have generally opposed increased federal control and federal spending, but more recently, Republican president George W. Bush used federal authority to hold schools accountable. Democrats have generally favored increased federal spending and regulation, but in recent years some Democratic members of Congress have raised questions about the use of federal power to require student testing and school accountability.[5]

Most clearly, race and ethnic conflicts have spilled over into the education arena. After all, it was *school* desegregation that was the focus of *Brown* v. *Board of Education,* and the civil rights movement of the 1960s concentrated much of its effort on the restructuring of school boundaries to minimize the educational effects of segregated residential neighborhoods. Racial and ethnic issues remain. Is further integration necessary? What is the best way to narrow racial and ethnic test-score gaps? How do

31

schools best teach students whose native tongue is not English? Are affirmative action policies constitutional? Surely, one cannot talk about cleavages in American education without acknowledging the relevance of one of the country's deepest divides.[6]

While all of the above-mentioned divisions are educationally relevant, our survey data suggest that none of them—with the possible exception of the racial and ethnic divide—impinge on school affairs with as much intensity as the teacher-public gap. We detect only modest divisions between parents of school-age children and other adults, between homeowners and renters, between the affluent and those of lesser means, between young and old, and between evangelical Protestants and others.[7] Even the much-discussed polarization between Democrats and Republicans does not rival that between teachers and the public.

Only the cleavages between whites and blacks and whites and Hispanics come close to rivaling in depth and range the disagreement between teachers and the public at large. Those divides, we argue, have the potential for complicating the teacher-public divide if school choice issues come to predominate. While minority opinion aligns with the views of teachers on such issues as education spending and some teacher prerogatives, on school choice issues the minority community and teachers are at odds. If those divides should gain in salience, they could strain relations between two constituencies—teachers' organizations and ethnic minorities—that have long been among the most reliable supporters of the Democratic Party.

The Broad Picture

The shape of each social cleavage is displayed in appendix table A-1. Column 1 shows the differences between the opinions of teachers and the public that were reported in chapter 2. In the next columns, the opinions of parents (2), homeowners (3), the affluent (4), and those who say that they have been "born again" (5) are each contrasted with the opinions of all other survey respondents who took a side on the issue. In subsequent columns, the comparisons are more focused: the views of the oldest third of respondents (6) are contrasted with the views of the youngest third; Democrats' views (7) are compared with those of Republicans (excluding independents), and African American (8) and Hispanic (9) opinions are each differentiated from white opinions (excluding Asians and others). In each case, it seems sensible to contrast the identified group with another equally defined group rather than with all other respondents, but the reader should note that such an analytic strategy may identify a sharper divide than if the group had been compared with the rest of the population (that is, for example, if the oldest cohort had been compared with all others instead of with the youngest cohort).[8]

The numerical values presented in table A-1 are the percentage-point differences in policy support between the identified group and the comparison group. Asterisks identify statistically significant differences, and a number shown in boldface print indicates majorities in opposition to one another. (Note that, as in chapter 2, all respondents who do not take a side on the issue are excluded from this analysis.)

Column 1 identifies the teacher-public gap. Note the several bolded numbers and the numerous asterisks. Together, they suggest a deep, broad divide. On nineteen of twenty-three issues, we identify a statistically significant difference between teacher opinion and that of the public as a whole. On nine of the twenty-three issues, a majority of teachers take a position opposite that of a majority of the general public. But even though that is the largest cleavage, others are not unimportant. Note especially columns 8 and 9, on the far right side of the table, which identify the racial and ethnic divides. Those columns, too, reveal many statistically significant differences.

The other social cleavages are more limited in scope and depth. For example, a majority of parents do not oppose a majority of the rest of the public on any issue. In no instance does a majority of affluent adults differ from a majority of those with less income and education. Those who identify themselves as born again differ from the majority of others on only one issue. On only three issues does a majority of homeowners disagree with majorities of the rest of the general public, while majorities of the oldest third and youngest third of our respondents disagree on only four issues.

Admittedly, one cannot interpret the size and significance of the divisions in school politics simply by counting up the number of survey items on which majorities of two groups oppose one another. Had we asked only questions about cultural questions—evolution, sex education, corporal punishment, and the like—a counting exercise would likely have found the divide between those with a born-again religious identity and the rest of the public to be fundamental. If only race-related issues are asked, that division would be highlighted. Our approach might be faulted for having included five questions on teacher employment policies and only three on cultural issues. But even though alternative selections of survey items can draw different pictures, the ones selected here reflect the policy debate in the first two decades of the twenty-first century. Up for discussion at every turn of the political cycle are taxes, spending, merit pay for teachers, teacher tenure, school vouchers, charter schools, testing, school and student accountability, affirmative action, mainstreaming, school prayer, and school discipline. Any survey that fails to touch on these issues would not be examining contemporary school politics. But to get a nuanced story of the social divides in education, we need to look at the specific issues that matter most to particular groups.

Parents, Homeowners, and the Affluent

Parents of school-age children have a clear interest in safe, effective, and attractive public schools for their children to attend.[9] For them, education can be expected to be a priority, and they may well have views not shared by those without children or those who no longer need to attend to their children's schooling. To give voice to their interests, many parents join the local PTA, and some join other, more militant parent advocacy organizations. In California, a "parent trigger" law enacted in 2010 gives parents at any underperforming school the power to initiate a political process that can bring about its reorganization as a charter school. The founder of the group known as Parent Revolution, which lobbies for parent trigger laws, defends them in these words: "Parents are the only ones without a conflict of interest when it comes to kids."[10] Similar policies have been proposed in the legislatures of twenty other states.

But are parents' views really all that different from those of the rest of the population? In our survey, only a few issues separate parents' opinions from those of others. Parents are more likely to back higher levels of spending, tax credits, and vouchers for all students (table A-1, column 2). But even as parents want to spend more money on schools and prefer a broader range of school choices, they stand especially opposed to affirmative action proposals that would have districts consider family income when assigning students to schools. While most of these differences imply that parents are somewhat more conservative than the rest of the public, the differences are not so polarizing as to pit a majority of parents against a majority of the rest of the public. On the remaining issues, parent opinion is not significantly different from that of adults without school-age children.

Homeowners, too, have a distinct set of interests when it comes to their local schools. Better than 40 percent of the cost of K–12 education is paid through local taxes, which typically means the property tax. That is one of the most visible taxes that a homeowner pays, and much—typically one-third or more—of that tax goes to fund local schools. By itself, that would seem to prompt homeowners to take a skeptical view of increases in school spending. In 1978 California voters passed Proposition 13 to limit property tax increases on existing homeowners to 2 percent each year. While the law remains on the books as the quintessential symbol of the anti-tax property owner, many of those who own their homes recognize that the quality of local schools affects their property values. It is possible that many homeowners are willing to pay higher taxes if they think that the money will be used effectively.

Overall, our survey data suggest that homeowners lean in the same direction as the California voters of 1978. They are significantly less likely than the public at large to support proposals to increase spending, raise taxes, or raise teacher pay (table A-1, column 3). They respond especially favorably to proposals to eliminate tenure and are more likely than the rest of the public to regard teacher unions as harmful. They are disproportionately opposed to such school choice policies as vouchers, tax credits, and online education, and they also resist affirmative action school-assignment policies.

In sum, homeowners respond as if they have a stake in the value of their property. They are suspicious of proposals that would raise taxes or waste local resources, and they favor policies that limit local services—such as local schools—to those who pay the local property tax. None of that is especially surprising. Still, the differences of opinion are rarely large enough that majorities of homeowners find themselves in opposition to a majority of the rest of the public.

The opinions of affluent Americans (whom we define as those with at least a bachelor's degree and income in the top 10 percent in their state) might be expected to differ from those of Americans with lesser means, because the affluent bear a heavier tax load and are more likely to have settled in an area where public schools perform well. When asked to evaluate the schools in their local community, 54 percent of affluent Americans but only 46 percent of the general public assign an "A" or "B" grade to those schools. And while 18 percent of the public give their local schools a "D" or an "F" grade, only 12 percent of the affluent do. Given their relatively high opinion of local schools, affluent Americans might be expected to be less supportive of school reform proposals.

Those who think that the United States is riddled with class conflict may be surprised to learn that the views of the affluent seem little different from those of the rest of the general public. On only three items do they hold distinctive positions: they are more supportive of allowing principals to hire uncertified teachers, more critical of teacher unions, and less enthusiastic about online education (table A-1, column 4). Virtually all of those differences are on the margins; on no issue does a majority of the affluent differ from a majority of the general public.

Cultural Divisions

Education is a hot spot for the culture wars. As Ralph Reed, the former head of the Christian Coalition, once said, "I would rather have a thousand school board members than one president [of the United States] and no school board members."[11] Yet if the divide between "born again" and other adults is real, it does not cut across many policy issues. School prayer is the most divisive one, with more than 90 percent of those who say that they have been "born again" favoring allowing time for silent prayer and reflection in school. Still, that policy is also supported by half of other adults. On two other issues—school vouchers and single-sex schooling—a double-digit difference is detected. But all other differences are quite modest in size or fall well short of statistical significance (table A-1, column 5).

Generational Conflict

"You can make a strong case that one dividing line has actually received too little attention. It's the line between young and old," wrote *New York Times* columnist David Leonhardt in the midst of the 2012 election campaign. The "young are generally losing out to the old," he continued. "Education spending—the area that the young say should be cut the least, polls show—is taking deep cuts."[12] Leonhardt's portrait undoubtedly reflects the conventional wisdom. It is widely thought that younger adults—the ones whose children need to be educated—favor more education spending and that they are also more liberal on social and cultural issues than their elders. Older adults are believed to think that government expenditures should be reserved for senior citizen programs and to cling to traditional ways of thinking.

There is some truth to those characterizations. Generational differences in policy preferences can be detected on numerous issues. But on only four items do a majority of the oldest third of our respondents (56 and older) hold a view opposed by the youngest third (adults not over the age of 41). Two-thirds of older citizens think that teacher unions are harmful, but less than one-half of younger adults do. Fewer than half of older Americans support government funding of private school tuition for low-income students, but 55 percent of younger Americans hold that opinion. More than three-quarters of young adults favor increased school spending; just short of half of older citizens are so inclined. A similar pattern holds for raising teacher pay (table A-1, column 6).

Other issues for which divisions exceeded 10 percentage points include providing tax credits to fund scholarships to private schools and raising taxes to pay for school spending, both of which had greater support among the young. The older group is more likely to favor policies that base teacher pay in part on student performance; test for grade promotions; require teachers to contribute more to their retirement benefits; separate out students with behavioral and emotional disabilities; and allow school prayer. In other words, the generational cleavage cuts across a wide range of issues, but it does not divide the groups consistently along liberal-conservative lines. The young are more liberal with regard to taxes, spending, and unions, but they also are more supportive of school choice.

Partisan Differences

Many of the policy debates in the United States are channeled through partisan differences. For example, other polls have found that Democratic and Republican voters divide over a universal health insurance program, tax cuts, a guest worker program for immigrants, U.S. troop presence in Afghanistan, and abortion.[13] Are education policies subject to a similar partisan divide? If so, are the disagreements between Republicans and Democrats so large that the cleavage is more significant than the one between teachers and the rest of the public? On Pennsylvania Avenue and Capitol Hill, the partisan divisions do seem deep and wide. Immediately upon his election to the presidency, Barack Obama called for termination of the school voucher program in Washington, D.C., one of the favorite initiatives of John Boehner, leader of the House Republicans. In 2012, the president criticized Republican governor Scott Walker of Wisconsin for enacting legislation that limited the collective bargaining rights of teacher unions and tightened teacher pension and health care benefits. Meanwhile, the Obama administration granted states a waiver from key provisions of No Child Left Behind, the federal accountability law that was the legislative pride of his Republican predecessor, George W. Bush. In early 2013, President Obama and his Democratic allies called for additional education spending even as Republicans supported automatic cuts as part of an across-the-board sequestration on non-entitlement spending.

Despite the partisan bickering, signs of bipartisanship surface episodically. The most notable, the Obama administration's school reform initiative Race to the Top, encouraged states to enact legislation that was favorable to both merit pay and charter schools, policies that historically have won more favor among Republican than among Democratic leaders.

Partisans within the Public

Do the divisions among partisan leaders translate into equally large divisions within the country? Or does the public ignore debates among state and national politicians when thinking through its own positions? In table A-1, column 7 shows the differences between respondents who identified with the Republican Party and those who identified with the Democratic Party.[14] On just four issues—teacher licensure, teacher unions, spending more on schools, and paying teachers higher salaries—do majorities of Republicans and Democrats differ from one another. However, substantial partisan differences are also apparent on teacher tenure, tax increases, and affirmative action.

On the remaining topics, partisan disagreement within the general public seems to be muted. On a number of prominent issues, including merit pay for teachers, school vouchers, charter schools, and other forms of school choice, there is hardly any difference of opinion between those who identify with one of the two major political parties. If partisan differences were the only factor shaping education politics, it would be a fairly placid scene.[15]

Influence of Party Leaders

Partisan identities and partisan differences over public issues may arise from common social and cultural influences that shape a person's point of view. But a number of psephologists have argued that partisan attachments are primary and opinions on public policy are derivative. They believe that partisan allegiances are learned early in life, reinforced by parental and neighborhood influences, and become almost as enduring a part of a person's identity as his or her religious and ethnic self-definition. Policy positions, in contrast, are lightly held, inconsistent, readily altered, and subject to the persuasion of party leaders.[16] If that is so, then one might expect party leaders to have considerable capacity to persuade their fellow partisans to their own preferred positions.

To examine that question, we performed a set of survey experiments in 2009 and 2010. Before being asked for their opinion on a policy issue, randomly selected respondents were told the position taken by the president, the most prominent partisan figure in the country, while other respondents were not given that information. If partisan cues powerfully shape public opinion, then the responses of Democrats informed of the president's position should shift toward that of the president (compared with responses of Democrats left uninformed) while the responses of informed Republicans should shift in the opposite direction (compared with responses of Republicans left uninformed)

The president is the public figure who has the greatest chance of shaping opinion along party lines. It is the president who has what Theodore Roosevelt called the "bully pulpit," the megaphone to which the media pay attention, magnifying every word that he says until, as Calvin Coolidge once said, "it weighs a ton." At the same time, a president's persuasiveness is likely to depend on his popularity with the general public. If a president is at the peak of his popularity, he may be able to persuade more than just his own partisans. If he is bogged down in controversy, his persuasive power may be limited, at best, to those who identify with his party.

We were able to consider the importance of presidential popularity in the two years in which we conducted these experiments because President Obama's popularity varied dramatically over the time period. In early 2009 Obama was a newly elected chief of state who enjoyed extraordinarily high popularity ratings; he had a nearly 70 percent approval rating throughout the spring of 2009.[17] By late spring 2010, however, his popularity had tumbled to below 50 percent. What's more, opinions of the president had by then become polarized. To be sure, Republicans have consistently given President Obama lower approval ratings than Democrats have, but when Obama first took office, approximately 40 percent of Republicans approved of his performance, along with 90 percent of Democrats. When we fielded our 2010 survey, roughly 80 percent of Democrats continued to approve of the president but only about one in ten Republicans did. Indeed, he was soon to face a severe electoral rebuke in the congressional elections held in November of that year. The changing political context could be expected to have a clear impact on the ability of the president to shape the views of both his own partisans and those of the opposing political party.

The results of the experiment, shown in table 3-1, are consistent with these expectations. In early 2009, direct information about the president's views on charter schools (which Obama favored) had the effect of shifting Democratic opinion in the direction of the president's by 14 percentage points. On vouchers, which the president opposed, Democratic opinion again shifted decisively toward the president's position—this time by no less than 25 percentage points—when information on the president's views was provided. Only on the merit pay issue (which Obama favored) was the shift in Democratic opinion among those directly informed a mere 7 percentage points—not large enough to be statistically significant.

All of that would seem to suggest that political leaders dramatically affect the opinions of their partisan followers—were it not for the fact that the shift among Republicans informed of the president's position was nearly as great—12, 21, and 6 percentage points in the same direction, respectively, on the same three issues. In other words, during his honeymoon period President Obama was able to shift opinion among Democrats and Republicans alike. Evidence of a presidential bully pulpit, yes; evidence of a distinctive partisan impact, no.

Table 3-1. *Impact of President Obama's Policy Stance on Opinions of Democrats and Republicans, 2009–10*[a]

Percentage difference

Issue/opinion	Republicans	Democrats	Difference
2009			
Allow charter schools (Obama supports)	+12	+14*	2
Use government funds for vouchers for low-income students (Obama opposes)	–21**	–24**	3
Use merit pay (Obama supports)	+6	+7	1
2010			
Use government funds for vouchers for low-income students (Obama opposes)	–4	–1	3
Use merit pay (Obama supports)	–11	+3	14
Require testing (Obama supports)	+1	+7**	6
Toughen standards and exams (Obama supports)	–2	+8**	10*

a. Table shows difference in policy positions of those informed and not informed of president's position. A positive sign identifies a shift toward greater support when respondents were informed; a negative sign identifies a shift toward less support when respondents were informed. Percentages in the difference column are absolute differences in the differential opinions of Republicans and Democrats in the informed and uninformed state.

** Statistically significant at the 0.05 level; * statistically significant at the 0.10 level.

A year later, when the president had lost a good deal of his popularity, his ability to shape the opinions of his fellow partisans was greatly reduced. In a stunning contrast to results just one year before, he was unable to alter opinions on vouchers at all. Nor was he any more effective on the merit pay issue. His only success with Democrats was in inducing them to express greater support for continued testing of students and for toughening of education standards. Even then, the shifts, while significant, were only 7 and 8 percentage points, respectively. The president's influence with Republicans also was minimal. On three of the four issues, opinion shifted away from the president among those who had learned his position, but none of the shifts were statistically significant.

Nonetheless, we see weak evidence that in the polarized political context of 2010 the president added to the partisan divide when he took positions on education issues. Partisan shifts were generally in opposite directions, and in one of the four instances, the widening partisan divide was statistically significant.

We conclude that political leaders, when acting within a polarized political context, contribute to the partisan divide. But when a political leader acquires great popularity, his actions dampen the differences. All of the changes are small to moderate in size, however. Partisanship may be deeply rooted in the history and psyche of Americans, but that does not mean that party leaders have a large capacity to differentially sway the opinions of rank-and-file partisans. Just as we see only a modest partisan cleavage on education issues, so we detect only a marginal impact of the most powerful of all partisan leaders—the president. Were we to search for the influence of a less visible public figure—say, the Speaker of the House of Representatives—it is likely that the impact would be even smaller.

Race, Politics, and the Democratic Party

Residential segregation sorts students into schools with relatively homogeneous ethnic and racial compositions. Minority groups are disproportionately concentrated in the nation's most poorly performing schools. A vast gap in achievement between those attending minority and white schools continues decades after legal segregation was ruled unconstitutional. Persistent differences in access to high-quality schools can be expected to generate disparate views concerning education reform.

As table A-1 shows, they clearly do. Indeed, the differences in opinion between whites and traditionally disadvantaged minorities are nearly as large and pervasive as the teacher-public divide. Significant differences between blacks and whites were detected on eleven of the twenty-three issues examined. On many of these issues, African Americans give more support to the teacher union agenda than whites do. More than whites, they favor higher spending, higher taxes, and increased teacher pay and see union influence more positively. They do not favor asking teachers to cover a higher share of the cost of health and retirement benefits along the lines enacted by Scott Walker in Wisconsin. Further, blacks more than whites favor keeping current teacher tenure practices. Yet African Americans are not especially favorable toward all teacher-supported policies. In particular, blacks are decidedly more in favor of school choice than whites. They disproportionately support means-tested vouchers, online learning for credit, and tax credits to fund scholarships to private schools. Finally, African Americans are far more supportive than whites of considering family income in order to foster diversity.

The pattern of opinion among Hispanics is similar. Like African Americans, Hispanics more than whites favor unions and think that more money should be spent on schools, taxes for schools should be higher, and teachers should be better paid; they also are less inclined to eliminate teacher tenure privileges. But on school choice questions, Hispanics, like African Americans, are more supportive than whites. More than whites, Hispanics favor school vouchers, credit for online coursework, and tax credits. On social diversity questions, they are much more likely to favor affirmative action and mainstreaming.

Race Conflict and the Teacher-Public Divide

The largest division remains the one between teachers and the public. Statistically significant differences are detected on nineteen of the twenty-three issues, and on nine of those nineteen, majorities of teachers disagree with a majority of the public at large. No other cleavage is so extensive or deep. Still, the racial and ethnic cleavage rivals the one between teachers and the public. Both are fundamental to education politics and policy. Yet much of the conventional wisdom focuses on other divisions that turn out to be quite modest—parents versus nonparents, homeowners versus renters, rich versus poor, old versus young, or "born again" versus those with other religious identities. At specific times and places, groups representing such interests may push school policy in directions that the public at large does not prefer. But in fact, they are a minor part of the political scene. School politics is dominated by two major social cleavages. The racial and ethnic divide is well known and has been thoroughly investigated over a range of scholarly traditions. It is the split between teachers and the public that is less understood.

Our results show that the divide between teachers and the public overlaps the divide between whites and minorities. On many topics teachers and minorities are aligned. Majorities of both disproportionately favor more education spending, higher teacher salaries, and teacher tenure. Both think that unions have done more good than harm. What's more, both teacher unions and civil rights groups are key constituencies of the Democratic Party. But the alliance between teachers and minority groups on these issues is offset by differences on affirmative action, merit pay, and especially school choice. The future of school politics could be shaped by tensions between two of the Democratic Party's most fervent political supporters, teacher unions and minority communities (a topic we explore in chapter 8). But first we need to examine the durability of the divide between teachers and the public. Does it disappear, for instance, when people are asked about schools and school policy in their local community instead of about school policy more generally? Does it change in size and scope when the public is provided specific information about schools? In the next chapters we turn our attention to these questions.

CHAPTER FOUR
My Back Yard

P<small>ERHAPS THE DIVIDE</small> between the general public and teachers shrinks when people are asked about schools in their local community. It could be that public thinking about local schools reflects direct experiences with the schools or is shaped by conversations with friends and neighbors, while its opinions about the nation's schools are shaped more by ideological speculation or by news reports about troubled schools in other places. People might endorse policies proposed for the nation as a whole that they would reject out of hand if proposed for local schools. Both teachers and the public may think differently about educational issues depending on the context in which proposals are made.

People often favor certain policies as long as they are not implemented in their immediate vicinity. The phenomenon is so widespread that it has acquired a catchphrase and acronym: the Not In My Back Yard (NIMBY) syndrome. People in Palo Alto, California, want high-speed rail, but not if it runs through their town. People in Nevada agree that low-level radioactive waste needs to be collected and safely deposited somewhere, but not at nearby Yucca Mountain. People on Cape Cod favor wind-generated energy, as long as the wind turbines are not placed in Nantucket Sound.

It is quite possible, perhaps even likely, that the NIMBY syndrome applies to education as well. Members of the public may want to fix the nation's schools by adopting strong policy innovations everywhere but in their own communities. The divide between teachers and the public may collapse when the framing of the issue shifts from the national to the local stage.

Grading Schools

Public evaluations of public schools at both the national and local level have been collected by two separate polling operations, the PDK/Gallup and Education Next polls, and data are available that cover an extended period of time. The results have consistently shown much higher evaluations of schools in respondents' local community than of schools in the nation as a whole.

PDK/Gallup Poll of the Public's Attitudes toward the Public Schools

Every year since 1981, the education journal *Phi Delta Kappan* (PDK) has asked a nationally representative sample of adults to evaluate both the nation's schools and the schools in the respondent's own community on the same "A" to "F" scale traditionally used to grade students. The PDK poll has shown fluctuations in voter evaluations over time (see figure 4-1), but between 1981 and 2001, on average, 25 percent of the public gave the nation's schools an "A" or a "B" while 22 percent gave them a "D" or an "F." The remaining half to three-fifths awarded a gentlemanly "C." In recent years, evaluations have been noticeably lower. For the six years from 2007 to 2012, only 20 percent of PDK respondents give the nation's schools one of the two highest marks. The percentage giving schools one of the two lowest grades climbs to 26 percent.

But if the respondents took a critical stance toward the nation's schools, the same cannot be said of their assessment of schools in their own community. PDK first began asking about local schools in 1974. Between that year and 2008, evaluations fluctuated from one period to the next (see figure 4-1), but 48 percent of those responding gave, on average, a grade of "A" or "B" to the schools in their community. During the most recent period, 2007 to 2012, the average is slightly higher—50 percent.[1]

Ednext *Poll*

Much the same results emerge from the *Ednext* poll administered between 2007 and 2012.[2] On average, 20 percent of the public give the nation's schools an "A" or a "B," while 25 percent hand them one of the two lowest grades; the remainder awarded schools a middling "C." When respondents are asked about local schools, 44 percent, on average, award them an "A" or a "B" and only 19 percent give them a "D" or an "F."

Figure 4-1. *Share of General Public Giving an "A" or a "B" Grade to the Nation's Schools and Local Schools, 1981–2012*[a]

Percent

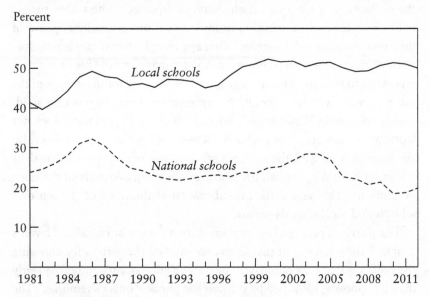

Source: Phi Delta Kappan annual survey, 1981–2012.
a. Percentages are three-year rolling averages, except those for the first and second years, which are one- and two-point averages. Those who said that they "didn't know" were removed from the observations.

In other words, almost half of the public rate local community schools as deserving one of the two highest grades, while only about one-fifth say that they deserve one of the two worst grades. In short, both surveys show local schools receiving twice as many high grades as the nation's schools receive.

The National-Local Puzzle

The much higher rating given by the public to local schools creates an enigma. Simply by substituting the words "in your community" for the words "in the nation as a whole," the survey generates a dramatically different set of evaluations from randomly chosen segments of the public.[3] Since the nation's schools are simply the sum of all the local schools in the country and opinions in a nationally representative survey are representative of attitudes toward local schools across the country, how can there be such a sharp difference?

Some solve the riddle in the same way that political scientists explain the dichotomy between evaluations of representatives in Congress and the evaluation of Congress itself. Surveys repeatedly show that people hold Congress as an institution in low esteem but generally approve of their own members of Congress.[4] That apparent inconsistency is not especially difficult to interpret, however. A voter may not hold his or her own representatives in the national legislature responsible for the defects of the institution as a whole. After all, the representative may be working assiduously to correct Washington's wrongs. Such an explanation does not work when thinking about schools. When respondents separately evaluate local schools and the nation's schools, the overall pattern of their responses should be similar, because they are being asked about the same institutions. Yet large differences between evaluations of the nation's schools and local schools persist.

The puzzle is perhaps best explained by what might be called "buyer's delight," the tendency of people to congratulate themselves for choosing the products that they purchase. "Buyer's delight" occurs more frequently than its opposite, identified by the familiar phrase "buyer's remorse." The latter happens when someone buys an expensive mattress only to discover that it is not as comfortable three nights in a row as it was in the salesroom. Buyer's remorse actually identifies exceptions, not the most common consumer response to purchases. Some complain about the "lemon" that they bought at the car dealer, but most people give their car more than a fair trial before complaining to others. Most of the time, people tend to rejoice over the things that they buy, if for no other reason than that doing so confirms their own good judgment. They proudly invite their friends to admire their new couch or chair, their new Samsung or Sony, or even their new Bosch or KitchenAid dishwasher. Only rarely do people admit—even to themselves—that their purchase did not turn out as well as expected.

So it is with the schools to which people send their children. It takes hard-nosed realists to admit that they are sending their child to a failing school or that the community in which they live has low-quality schools. Even schools officially identified by the government as failing find themselves quite capable of mobilizing parental support for their continued operation. For example, in New York City in 2010, the school chancellor tried to close nineteen schools that had been identified as especially ineffective, but prolonged demonstrations and lawsuits delayed the closures for more than a year. In Chicago, teacher union president Karen Lewis mobilized parental support for her campaign against closures of low-performing schools.

So it is not surprising that parents give local schools a higher grade than do nonparents, despite the fact that the two groups evaluate the nation's schools in similar terms. For parents, it is especially important to rejoice over this particular purchase. Fifty-seven percent of parents grant their local schools an "A" or a "B," while only 26 percent say that the nation's schools deserve the same grades.

Schools and Other Local Institutions

Although local schools are considered superior to the nation's schools, the public is not particularly satisfied with them. Less than a majority of the public gave the local schools anything better than a grade of "C." That does not compare well with the ratings that people give to other local institutions. In 2008 the public was asked to evaluate the local post office and the local police on the same A-to-F scale used to judge schools. While only 40 percent of the public give schools one of the two highest grades, no less than 70 percent say the local post office deserved an "A" or a "B." Enthusiasm for the local police department is only slightly weaker: 64 percent say that it deserves one of the two highest grades. Furthermore, schools are much more likely to get one of the two lowest grades. Twenty-five percent of the public judge schools to be worthy of no more than a "D" or an "F," while one of those grades is given by only about 10 percent of the public to the post office and the police department. In sum, the public thinks local schools are considerably better than the nation's schools, but they still have reservations about the quality of local schools relative to that of other local public services.

Teacher Evaluations of Schools

Teachers evaluate public schools more generously than the public does. According to PDK polls administered between 1995 and 1999, 29 percent of the teachers, on average, said that the nation's schools deserve an "A" or a "B." On three occasions (in 2008, 2011, and 2012), *Ednext* found that, on average, 32 percent of the teachers, but only 20 percent of the public, award the nation's schools one of the two highest grades

Table 4-1. *Grades Given by General Public and Teachers to Nation's Schools and Local Schools, 2007–12*[a]

Percent

Schools/grade	General public	Teachers
Nation's schools		
A or B	20	32
C	58	52
D or F	25	16
Local schools		
A or B	44	62
C	37	25
D or F	19	13

a. Average assessment over the time period. Responses to *Ednext* surveys, 2007–12. National question was posed to the general public each year, 2007–12, and to teachers each year, 2008–12. Local question was posed to the general public in 2007, 2008, 2011, and 2012 and to teachers in 2008, 2011, and 2012. See appendix B for the wording of the questions.

(see table 4-1). Teachers are also reluctant to give the nation's schools one of the two lowest grades: only 10 percent of teachers did so in the PDK poll conducted in the 1990s. More recently, when surveyed by *Ednext,* just 16 percent of teachers but 25 percent of the public hand out a "D" or an "F."

The difference between teachers and the public is even sharper when it comes to evaluating schools in their own community. When PDK pollsters intermittently asked teachers to assess local schools, no less than 62 percent of them, on average, awarded local schools one of the two highest grades. The more recent *Ednext* polls also find that more than 60 percent of the teachers gave local schools the higher grades (see table 4-1). Meanwhile, only 7 percent of teachers handed out one of the two worst grades in the earlier PDK poll, and just 13 percent reach that judgment in the more recent *Ednext* polls.[5] In other words, the NIMBY phenomenon is especially pronounced for teachers. When the focus shifts from the national to the local level, the percentage of high evaluations increases by 30 points among teachers but by only 20 percentage points among the public.

Teachers also have a more favorable view of local schools relative to other local institutions than the public does. According to the 2008 poll, 61 percent of teachers thought that local schools deserve an "A" or a

"B," about the same as the 64 percent willing to give local police one of those grades. Some 77 percent of teachers think equally well of the postal service. At the other end of the scale, 16 percent of teachers say that local schools are so bad that they deserve a "D" or an "F," considerably more than the approximately 5 percent of teachers who grade the local postal service and police department that harshly.

In other words, when it came to assessing schools, both the public and teachers grade local schools more generously than the nation's schools. Still, there is no attenuation of the public-teacher divide. On the contrary, teacher assessments of local schools are even more favorable than those granted by the general public. One should not be especially surprised by that finding. If "buyer's delight" is at work, then one would also expect to find "seller's delight." Those who sell Fords are likely to believe in their product every bit as much as those who sell Cadillacs. Unless they get very strong signals to the contrary, employees have powerful psychological and economic incentives to believe that their product is worth the price that the customer is being asked to pay. It is hard for anyone other than a very unhappy teacher to admit to working at anything less than a good school.

NIMBY Politics: Does It Exist?

The different assessments of national and local schools give rise to several questions: Does the public want reform in its own back yard? Or does it want one thing for the nation's schools and something else locally? How about teachers? Does the divide between the public and the teaching profession intensify or dissipate as the focus shifts from national to local reforms?

To see whether the divide between teacher and public opinion over school policies fades when people are asked about adopting policies in their own community, we divide those surveyed into randomly chosen segments, one segment receiving a question about adopting a policy nationally and the other a question about policy adoption in the local community. For example, respondents in one segment are asked whether they favor the formation of charter schools in general terms, while those in the second are asked whether they support or oppose the formation of charter schools "in your community." In another example, the first group is asked about offering tenure to teachers "across the country," while the second is asked about offering tenure to teachers "in your local schools." This experiment is repeated for nineteen of the policy questions discussed in chapter 2. (See appendix B for the exact wording of each question.)

In only a few instances does the public respond in a NIMBY-like fashion (see table 4-2). Responses to twelve of the nineteen questions do not differ significantly when questions are framed in a local rather than a national context. Among those who have opinions, 57 percent think that principals nationwide should be able to hire college graduates as teachers even if the graduates do not have their teaching credential; the same percentage take that position with regard to local school principals. Merit pay for teachers is favored by just short of 65 percent of the public whether the policy question is asked within the national or local context. Seventy percent of the public support the creation of charter schools when asked about the topic in general terms, and 75 percent favor creation of the schools in their own community. That difference is not statistically significant. Indeed, public opinion does not depend in any significant way on whether the respondent is asked to think about the issue in a national or local context on accountability items; on school choice questions, including questions on vouchers, charters, and tax credits; on merit pay and teacher unions; and on mainstreaming the disabled.

Even when evidence of NIMBY thinking does appear, the magnitude is modest. The biggest difference has to do with increasing taxes for school expenditures. The public is more willing to back tax increases in the national (35 percent) than the local context (28 percent). Our data do not reveal exactly why respondents are less supportive of higher local taxes to fund public schools in their own district than they are of higher taxes to fund public schools around the nation. Perhaps they believe higher local taxes will more assuredly increase their own tax bill, while higher taxes around the nation would come out of someone else's pocket. Perhaps they feel their local schools perform adequately at current revenue levels, while schools around the nation are in greater need of assistance. Perhaps they feel it is unfair that they should increase their local burden without more assistance from state or federal authorities. Whatever the reason, they are more hesitant to take on higher taxes in their own districts than to see

Table 4-2. *Comparison of General Public and Teacher Opinions on Issue as It Pertains to Nation's Schools and Local Schools, 2011*

Percent

Issue/opinion	General public			Teachers		
	National	Local	Difference	National	Local	Difference
Teacher policy						
Use merit pay	64	65	1	20	20	0
Use merit tenure	74	80	6**	34	33	–1
Allow flexible hiring	57	57	0	32	31	–2
Eliminate tenure	70	64	–6**	37	31	–6
Teacher unions are harmful	56	54	–2	35	23	–12**
School choice						
Expand choice with universal vouchers	64	61	–3	40	32	–8
Use government funds for means-tested vouchers	50	48	–2	36	34	–2
Allow charter schools	70	75	5	54	50	–4
Allow tax credit–funded scholarships	70	70	0	54	44	–10**
Allow online courses	65	70	5**	58	70	12**
Accountability						
Use test for grade promotion	86	86	0	71	67	–4
Require graduation test	86	88	2	75	75	0
Taxes and spending						
Increase spending	65	59	–6*	70	71	1
Raise taxes	35	28	–7**	50	42	–8*
Raise teacher pay	55	52	–3	82	66	–16**
Increase teacher share of benefit costs	64	64	0	28	26	–2
Cultural issues						
Allow single-sex schools	59	54	–5*	70	66	–5
Diversity						
Use family income to assign students	37	36	–1	35	42	8
Separate classes for disturbed students	65	64	–1	64	65	0

* Statistically significant at the 0.10 level; ** statistically significant at the 0.05 level.

taxes rise across the nation. Responses follow a similar pattern when respondents are asked about increasing education spending in the national
(65 percent support) as opposed to the local context (59 percent support).
Nor is the public quite so enthusiastic about the single-sex schooling
option within their own communities. However, on two other items—
modifying tenure provisions and online learning—the public is more supportive of policy proposals framed in the local context.

NIMBYism among the Affluent and Minority Groups

Although the general public seldom indulges in NIMBYism, it's possible
that key subgroups—the affluent, say, or minority groups—think differently, depending on whether a question is framed in the national or local
context. The affluent are especially at risk of developing the NIMBY syndrome because they draw a strong distinction between the nation's schools
and their own. Only 15 percent of the affluent say that the nation's schools
deserve an "A" or "B," while 55 percent think that their local schools do.
And, indeed, NIMBYism is detected in the responses that the affluent
gave to four items. They are 12 percentage points less likely to support
increases in salaries for teachers when the question is locally framed; their
support for tax increases for educational expenditures drop by 11 percentage points. And they are 21 percentage points less enthusiastic about
vouchers and 8 percentage points less supportive of tax credits when asked
whether those measures should be adopted locally. While no other statistically significant differences are detected, affluent communities might be
fruitful places to search, if NIMBY hypocrites are to be hunted down.

African Americans are less likely than the public as a whole to give their
local schools a high grade. Just 38 percent thought that their local schools
deserve an "A" or a "B," 8 percentage points less than the public as a
whole. By comparison, Hispanics are happy with their schools. No less
than 58 percent award their local schools one of the two highest grades.

When it came to policy issues, minority opinion does not vary much by
the context in which the questions were posed. But there are some exceptions. Like the public as a whole, Hispanics are less supportive of tax
increases when asked about the local context, and African Americans are
less supportive of pay increases for teachers when the question is set
within a local framework. Both ethnic groups, like the public as a whole,
are more likely to favor teacher tenure in the local than the national con-

text. While some distinctions between the national and the local contexts are drawn by both African American and Hispanic respondents, overall it is hard to find a clear NIMBY syndrome among minority respondents.

NIMBYism among Teachers

Among teachers, national or local framing of a question generates significant differences in responses for five of the nineteen items in table 4-2. But only one item reflected what might be called a classic example of NIMBYism: teachers are less likely to favor tax credits to fund scholarships for low-income students in the local than in the national context. Otherwise, they are more favorable to tax increases and increases in teacher salaries if the question is posed in the national context, quite the opposite of what one might expect from the self-interested teacher. They are also more willing to have students take online courses when the question is posed in the local context. Most significant, they are more likely to think that teacher unions are harmful if the question is posed in the national rather than local context. Evidently some teachers like their own union, perhaps because it provides job protection, but think that the stance that the unions have taken nationally has gone too far. Still, there is little evidence that NIMBYism has either opened or closed the teacher-public divide.

Not a NIMBY Syndrome

Despite the fact that people had a more favorable opinion of their local schools than of the nation's schools, a strong NIMBY syndrome on education policy questions does not exist. It is true that the public is less likely to favor higher taxes and spending and higher teacher salaries when the issue is posed in the local context, suggesting an inclination to spend more taxpayer dollars if others are thought to be paying the bill. Otherwise, a majority of the public favors an education reform for the local area if they favor the idea for the nation. Other than a reluctance among the affluent to support local school choice, we find no strong examples of NIMBYism with respect to education reforms. Even teachers take much the same position in the local as in the national context.

If the public is not getting the policies that it says it wants, it is not because of an internally inconsistent set of opinions favoring one thing for the nation's schools and something else for the local community. Any unresponsiveness in the education system to public opinion, we suggest, is the work of the education iron triangle. But perhaps the picture changes when both teachers and the public have more information about current expenditures on education and current school performance. Those are the topics that we pursue in the next two chapters.

CHAPTER FIVE

Information Corrodes

IRON REMAINS PERPETUALLY strong in the absence of oxygen, but when exposed to the open air, it begins to rust and disintegrate. In politics, the iron triangle survives by means of closed doors, secret meetings, quiet negotiations, and unidentified financial contributions. When the public becomes better informed, fresh air corrodes the iron triangle. As the nation witnessed the spectacular collapse of some of its largest financial houses in 2008, calls for more financial regulation increased. The Dodd-Frank Wall Street Reform and Consumer Protection Act soon followed. Similarly, when the public learned of serious damage to beaches and wildlife in the wake of British Petroleum's Deepwater Horizon oil spill in 2010, public support for offshore drilling declined and demand for environmental protection increased. When Solyndra, a politically well-connected and government-assisted solar energy company, found itself the subject of headlines reporting financial troubles and questionable dealings, Congress put federal subsidies for alternative energy companies under tighter scrutiny. In each of these cases, greater public focus disrupted the normally cozy dealings between policymakers and client groups. But does information have the same impact on the education iron triangle?

"Sunlight is said to be the best of disinfectants," reform-minded jurist Louis Brandeis once wrote, and information has always been among the levers that education reformers have pushed to build public support for their cause. Horace Mann, recognized today as the progenitor of the modern public school system, shifted power from local school boards to state education officials in the 1840s by first gathering and disseminating education statistics. When the U.S. Office of Education was established in

1870, its primary purpose was to collect information about the condition of education in the states and territories. Its commissioner asked districts to report the number of students enrolled by grade level, the numbers of teachers and other employees, expenditures on a wide range of school functions, and much more. Even after the Office of Education became a full-fledged cabinet-level department in 1980, serving as chief information officer for the nation's school systems continues to be one of its core responsibilities.[1]

In recent years, demands for school reform have been propelled by evidence that U.S. students trail their peers abroad as well as by the wide gaps between the performances of white and minority students within the United States. With the passage of the No Child Left Behind Act (NCLB), every school district is required to report annually the aggregate math and reading performance of students in each of its schools, both overall and within subgroups defined by race and income. In many schools, student proficiency levels have been found to be alarmingly deficient. Advocacy groups have relied heavily on that information to make the case for school reform through research articles, commission reports, high-profile television and film documentaries, online databases that rate the performance of students in local districts relative to that of students in other countries, and even Super Bowl advertisements.[2] In light of such efforts, is it possible that information about American schools is so widely available that the provision of any new data would leave public opinion—and the divide between teachers and the general public on education issues—unchanged? That is the question that motivates the analyses in this chapter and the next.

Gross Underestimation of Costs

Surprisingly, given the collection of detailed information on school expenditures by the U.S. Department of Education, the members of the American public have a poor grasp of the per-pupil cost of education in their local school district or the average salary paid to public school teachers in their state. They grossly underestimate both. As a result, their views on whether more money is needed and whether salaries should be increased change dramatically when they are provided with this basic information. For teachers, the impact of this information is not as great.

School Spending Knowledge

In 2007, we asked respondents to estimate the average amount of money spent per child each year in the school district in which they lived. Half of the sample was asked to estimate costs without any help or guidance. The other half, randomly chosen, was reminded that districts' costs included "teacher and administrator salaries, building construction and maintenance, extracurricular activities, transportation, etc.," thereby encouraging respondents to think expansively when making their estimates. At the time that the questions were posed, the only reliable, publicly available information on per-student expenditure in each school district was for the school year ending in 2005. For that year, the U.S. Department of Education reported that the average per-pupil expenditure was nearly $10,400 in the districts in which the respondents in our sample resided.[3]

THE PUBLIC

The American public is hopelessly uninformed about school districts' fiscal realities. When respondents are left without any guidance, the average estimate is just over $4,200 per student, or roughly 60 percent below actual spending levels in their district. Reminding people of the range of expenses that school districts face does improve their assessments, but not by much. For members of the group told about the range of costs that need to be covered, the estimate increases to just $5,300, still almost 50 percent below actual per-pupil spending levels in their district.

To see whether our 2007 survey was a fluke, in 2012 we again asked the public to estimate per-pupil expenditures in their district. By that time, average per-pupil spending in the districts included in our survey had increased to approximately $12,500. The public recognized that expenditures had increased, as the 2012 average estimate comes to about $6,600, up from $4,200 in 2007. Nonetheless, the average estimate is still only 52 percent of actual expenditures.

TEACHERS

Teachers also underestimate per-pupil expenditures in their district, although not by as much. In 2012, they estimate those expenditures to be just over $7,500, or 60 percent of actual expenditures. Though better informed than the public, they hardly have a good sense of the costliness of the enterprise in which they are engaged. This finding suggests that any difference of opinion between teachers and the general public on spending matters is more likely to be a function of teachers' vested interest in public education funding than of their greater familiarity with school finance.

Information Matters

To see whether public opinion concerning increased expenditures changes when respondents are informed of actual levels of spending in their local district, we divide the sample into two parts. Half of the sample is left uninformed of the true level of recent expenditures in their district, while the other half is given the amount reported by the U.S. Department of Education for the most recent year that information was available.[4] ("Uninformed" is to be understood in the technical sense that respondents were not specifically told the level of current spending in their district at the time the question was posed. Some respondents may have acquired this information from some other source.) These experiments were conducted in 2008, 2010, and 2012 (and also in 2013, as reported in the next chapter).

THE PUBLIC

The impact of information on the public's preferences for more spending is quite dramatic. Combining responses across these years, support for increased expenditures in local districts drops 18 percentage points, to just 38 percent, among respondents who are told how much is currently being spent.[5] The effect of accurate information also influences the public's confidence that increased spending will improve student learning. We posed that question in 2008 and again in 2010. Combining the results for the two years reveals that 64 percent of the general public, when not informed, say they are confident that more spending would improve student learning in their district, but that figure falls by 17 percentage points when they are provided with information about current expenditures.[6]

TEACHERS

At 66 percent, support among uninformed teachers for increased expenditures is 10 percentage points higher than among the uninformed general public. Teacher support shifts downward by 17 percentage points when teachers are told about actual expenditure levels, approximately the same impact as for the general public. Teachers are also less confident that additional expenditures would enhance school performance once they are told of current expenditure levels. Only 55 percent of teachers informed of current expenditures express confidence in the prospects for additional money to improve performance, again a difference of 17 percentage points between them and the uninformed group of teachers.

Taxes

From the results reported above, one might conclude that more information about school expenditures does not exacerbate the teacher-public divide. But in 2012 we altered the experiment by asking four different variations of the question. Groups A and B were asked the questions about school expenditures just discussed. Group C was asked the following question: "Do you think taxes to fund public schools should increase, decrease, or stay the same?" For group D, we worded the question as follows: "According to the most recent information available, $ [current expenditure per student] is being spent per child attending public schools in your district. Do you think taxes to fund public schools should increase, decrease, or stay the same?" In short, whereas respondents in groups A and B were simply asked about spending, respondents in groups C and D were asked about their attitudes toward the source of funds for that spending.

THE PUBLIC

As shown in figure 5-1, the percentage of general public respondents favoring increased school spending shifts sharply downward both when it is made clear that such an increase entails paying more taxes and when it is informed of current education expenditures. When neither taxes nor current expenditures are mentioned, 63 percent of respondents favor higher spending, but when both taxes are mentioned and current expenditures are provided, the impact is dramatic: just 24 percent say that more spending is desirable. That is a shift of no less than 39 percentage points induced simply by informing respondents of current spending levels and reminding them that higher expenditures imply higher taxes.[7]

Figure 5-1. *General Public and Teacher Opinion in Favor of Taxes and Spending, with and without Information, 2012*[a]

Percentage favoring increased . . .

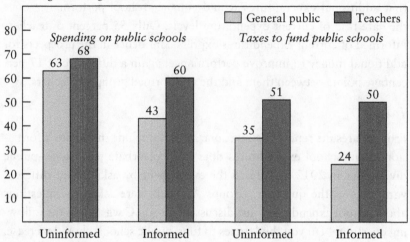

a. See appendix B for wording of the questions. Informed respondents are those who were told the level of per-pupil expenditures in their local district.

TEACHERS

The teaching force also becomes less enthusiastic about spending increases when both informed of current levels of spending and asked whether taxes should be raised for the purpose. For teachers, the drop is from 68 percent to 40 percent. That's a decline of 28 percentage points, but it is still significantly less than the change in opinion among the general public.[8] One can conclude that it is to the advantage of those inside the education iron triangle to separate discussions of education spending from talk about tax increases and to minimize public knowledge of current expenditure levels.

Teacher Salary Knowledge

When it comes to teacher salaries, the significance of information for the teacher-public divide is even greater. Teachers have a reasonably clear picture of average salaries within their state, while the public is almost as confused as it is with respect to school expenditures in general. For that reason, providing information that corrects the knowledge imbalance between those inside and those outside the iron triangle has an especially large impact.

THE PUBLIC

The American Federation of Teachers (AFT) collects information on teacher salaries by state, although it excludes from its report the sizable share of the teacher compensation package comprising health care benefits, pensions, life insurance, disability insurance, and other benefits. According to the AFT, in 2005 the national average salary for teachers came to a little more than $47,600.[9] When asked (in 2007) about the average teacher salary in their state, members of the public offers a significantly smaller figure— less than $33,100.[10] In other words, the public underestimates average teacher salaries by 30 percent ($14,500). By 2012, the most recent AFT estimate of teacher salaries nationwide climbed to an average of $56,000 a year. But when asked to hazard a guess as to what teachers were making, the public clocks in at $35,920 on average, 35 percent below the actual level. Despite all the controversy over teacher compensation reform in Chicago, Wisconsin, Indiana, and elsewhere, public knowledge about actual teacher compensation levels eroded slightly between 2007 and 2012.

TEACHERS

Members of the teaching force thought that salaries in their state came to $43,997—21 percent below actual levels, an underestimate that is considerably less than the 35 percent underestimate among the general public. Although each teacher's salary may be quite different from the average, it is not surprising that the teaching force has a better sense than the public at large of salaries across the state.

Information Matters Again

Between 2008 and 2011, we conducted three survey experiments related to teacher salaries that were similar to those that we conducted for school expenditures in general. A random half of those surveyed were told the average teacher salary in their state before we asked them whether they thought that teacher salaries should increase, remain the same, or be cut. The other half were not given that information. When the public was provided with information on current salaries, its support for higher ones drops 14 percentage points, to 46 percent.[11]

In 2008, we checked to see whether the effect of information varies with the degree of satisfaction of respondents with their local public schools. Among those who earlier in the same survey had assigned the schools in their community a grade of A or B, the provision of information on actual teacher salaries reduces support by just 9 percentage points, to 60 percent. Among respondents who assign their schools a grade of C or lower, information reduces support by a whopping 18 percentage points. In other words, information has the greatest impact when the public is least satisfied with the status quo.

By 2012, the debate over teacher compensation had intensified. The federal government was encouraging the introduction of merit pay plans, many states were clamping down on teacher pensions, and the conflict between teacher unions and Wisconsin governor Scott Walker had become a national issue. In that context, the results of our teacher salary experiment are even starker than in earlier years. When the public is provided with information about actual levels of compensation, its support for higher salaries tumbles dramatically, falling 28 percentage points to a low of 36 percent.[12]

TEACHERS

Information about actual salaries has a smaller impact on teachers' desire for further increases. Between 2008 and 2011, support among the informed group, at 76 percent, is only 7 percentage points less than among the uninformed.[13] In 2012, support is, again, 11 percentage points lower among the informed, only somewhat larger than in the preceding years.

In short, better information widens the gap between those inside and outside the education iron triangle. The more that the public knew about teacher salaries, the less it agrees with public employees that they should be compensated at a higher level. Information plays an especially critical role when political confrontations take place. Still, there is no sign that public knowledge about actual levels of teacher compensation has improved despite the multiple public disputes in recent years, perhaps because the media focuses more on the personalities and tactics of the contestants than on the substance of the issues contested.

The Great Unknowns

It is not just financial matters that stump many American citizens. A substantial share avoids taking a clear position one way or another on many policy issues if given the opportunity to take a neutral one, perhaps because they lack enough information to decide. Of the twenty-three policy questions discussed in chapter 2, respondents could choose a neutral position on eighteen. More than 25 percent of the public took the neutral position on thirteen of those questions (table 5-1). By contrast, on only one issue—single-sex education—did the portion of teachers taking a neutral position exceed 25 percent.[14] In sum, the teaching force is more decided than the public in general in its opinions on education matters. That is hardly surprising, given that teachers are more likely to have a personal stake in the issues and more closely follow the debates surrounding them. Indeed, when asked how much attention they pay to issues involving education, the share of teachers answering "a great deal" or "quite a bit" is 84 percent, while just 36 percent of the public as a whole respond accordingly.[15]

Admittedly, failure to take one side or another on a policy question is not by itself proof that the public is poorly informed. It is possible that most of the public has plenty of information on the seventeen policy issues listed in table 5-1 and has given them considerable thought but has nonetheless concluded that the weights of the arguments, pro and con, are so balanced that it makes no sense to prefer one side over the other. For most of those eighteen issues, we cannot rule out that possibility, however unlikely it might be. But on one school policy, charter schools, we ask a series of questions that enable us to estimate more precisely the American public's knowledge base.

Charter School Knowledge

Minnesota enacted the first charter school law in 1990, and more than forty states followed suit in the ensuing two decades. Charter schools are public schools of choice that are privately managed under a renewable performance contract that exempts them from many of the state and collective bargaining constraints that district schools face. As public schools, they cannot charge tuition or have a religious affiliation. If they have facilities available, they must accept any student who wishes to attend. If oversubscribed, they must choose among applicants by means of a lottery.

Table 5-1. *Share of the General Public and Teachers Taking a Neutral Position, 2011*[a]

Percent

Issue/opinion	General public	Teachers	Difference between public and teachers
Teacher policy			
Use merit pay	26	9	−17*
Use merit tenure	26	9	−17*
Allow flexible hiring	26	9	−17*
Eliminate tenure	31	11	−20*
Teacher unions are harmful	34	16	−18*
School choice			
Expand choice with universal vouchers	23	15	−8*
Use government funds for means-tested vouchers	26	16	−10*
Allow charter schools	39	16	−23*
Allow tax credit–funded scholarships	29	14	−15*
Allow online courses	27	17	−10*
Accountability			
Require annual testing	19	13	−6
Use common standards/test	NA	NA	NA
Use test for grade promotion	19	16	−3
Require graduation test	16	12	−4
Taxes and spending			
Increase spending	NA	NA	NA
Raise taxes	NA	NA	NA
Raise teacher pay	NA	NA	NA
Increase teacher share of benefit costs	33	20	−13*
Cultural issues			
Allow single-sex schools	43	33	−10*
Grant principal final disciplinary authority	NA	NA	NA
Allow time for silent prayer	28	25	−3
Diversity			
Use family income to assign students	34	19	−15*
Separate classes for disturbed students	24	9	−15*

a. NA indicates that a neutral response category was not available for the relevant item. See appendix B for the wording of the questions. Silent prayer and disciplinary authority questions are from the 2008 survey. Estimates use national population weights in order to facilitate tests for statistically significant differences across the two groups.

* Statistically significant at the 0.05 level.

Charter schools typically receive somewhat less government funding for each student that they enroll than traditional public schools in their area, although some charter schools succeed in raising charitable contributions to offset (or even reverse) the shortfall. Proponents hail charter schools as a source of much-needed innovation in public education and cite the success of a growing number of charters in producing impressive academic gains for students in many of the nation's most troubled urban centers. Critics allege that they drain much-needed resources from school districts and note the wide variation in the performance of charter schools as a whole.

Despite the controversy, charter schools have been endorsed by presidents Clinton, Bush, and Obama and today are attended by nearly 5 percent of all public school children nationwide, although they are concentrated in relatively few places, such as Arizona, California, Florida, and Washington, D.C. Among members of the public who chose a side in this debate, over 70 percent are favorably disposed. Yet a large segment of the public remain unwilling or unable to say whether it favors or opposes the formation of charter schools. In 2012, fully 41 percent of the public took the neutral position when given an opportunity to do so. Clearly, a large plurality of the American public felt they did not know enough to come out for or against public schools.

THE PUBLIC

To see just how much the public knows about charter schools, we ask (in 2012) a series of questions: Can charter schools charge tuition? May they hold religious services? Do they receive more, less, or about the same government funding as traditional public schools? Are they required to admit students by lottery if more apply than can be accepted? The lack of knowledge about such basic characteristics of charter schools is quite remarkable. The percentage of public respondents who say that they do not know the answers to those questions varies between 44 percent and nearly 60 percent, depending on the question (see table 5-2). Of those who do respond, nearly as many and sometimes more respondents give the wrong answer as the correct one. For example, 32 percent of the public incorrectly report that charter schools can charge tuition, while just 24 percent say that they cannot. Still, public knowledge about charter

Table 5-2. *General Public and Teacher Knowledge about Charter Schools, 2012*

Percent

Question/response	General public	Teacher
To the best of your knowledge, can charter schools hold religious services?		
Correct (No, they cannot hold religious services)	22	38
Incorrect	20	30
Don't know	59	39
To the best of your knowledge, can charter schools charge tuition?		
Correct (No, they cannot charge tuition)	24	46
Incorrect	32	30
Don't know	44	24
In general, do charter schools receive more, less, or the same amount of government funds for each student enrolled than do traditional public schools?		
Correct (They receive less than public schools)	20	19
Incorrect	31	54
Don't know	49	28
To the best of your knowledge, when more students apply to a charter school than there are spaces available, can the school pick the students they want or must they hold a lottery?		
Correct (They must hold a lottery)	28	45
Incorrect	22	26
Don't know	51	29

schools seems to have increased in recent years. Between 2007 and 2012, the percentage of the public that correctly answered the questions about religious services and tuition increased by 7 percentage points and 12 percentage points, respectively.[16]

TEACHERS

The teachers in our survey are much less likely—around 20 percentage points less likely, in fact—to say that they do not know the answer to our factual questions or to say that they neither support nor oppose charters. Also, they are much more likely to answer questions correctly (see table 5-2). Only in one instance—the funding of charter schools—are teachers more likely to give an erroneous answer. They think that charters typically receive more government support than they actually do. Given the stake of public school teachers in the outcome of the charter debate, they have evidently taken the time to become more informed about the nature of this new educational institution—or the information crosses their path more frequently in the ordinary course of their working day.

The Impact of Information

In 2008 we investigated the effect of uncertainties and misperceptions about charter schools on the public's willingness to endorse them. We informed one randomly chosen group of respondents that charter schools "cannot charge tuition and they cannot provide religious instruction" before probing their support. We asked a second group their opinion of charter schools without first providing that information.

Support among liberals and conservatives varies depending on whether they were given information about charter policy.[17] Among the uninformed, 72 percent of conservatives and 61 percent of liberals support charter schools. But when they are told that charter schools are tuition free and secular, support among conservatives holds steady at 71 percent while it increases among liberals by 10 percentage points, to the same high level. Apparently, opposition by some liberals to charter schools is due to misperception of their characteristics.

Among the public as a whole, the provision of information leaves the level of support for charter schools unchanged, with just over 70 percent of those who offer an opinion expressing support, because the increment in support among liberals is offset by a decline among self-identified moderates. Similarly, being told that charter schools are tuition free and secular has no impact on support among teachers. In short, providing respondents with information about charter schools does not change the overall level of support for charters, but it shifts their base of political support in a more liberal direction. From that shift it might be concluded that this particular reform may win increasing support among liberals. Indeed, the Obama administration's visible advocacy of charter schools in recent years may indicate that this process is already under way.[18] Yet the provision of information does not alter the magnitude of the divide on the charter school issue between the general public and teachers, who remain markedly less enthusiastic about, if still open to, the idea.

High School Graduation Rates

In today's economy, a high school diploma is generally regarded as the minimum level of educational attainment a student must reach if he or she is to be at all successful in the workforce—and in many other aspects of life. Those who do not obtain a high school diploma have lower wages, are more likely to be unemployed, are more likely to head one-parent households, and are less well off in numerous other ways. So important is the high school diploma to success that President Barack Obama has urged states to raise the age of compulsory schooling to 18 years, when students typically graduate; approximately half the states now set that age at 16. But does the American public have any idea as to what percentage of high school students graduate on time? And once they are given accurate information on the topic, what impact does it have on their evaluation of schools? The answers may be surprising to those who think that the public has a self-indulgent view of the nation's school system.

According to the U.S. Department of Education, in 2008 approximately 75 percent of students graduated from high school within four years of entering ninth grade.[19] Some of those who do not graduate on time are nonetheless able to earn their high school diploma; a sizable percentage successfully pass a test that allows them to claim the General Educational Development credential (GED), which is marketed by those who offer the GED test as demonstrating knowledge equivalent to that of a high school graduate. However, economists who have looked into the matter have generally concluded that the market value of a GED is much less than that of a standard diploma.

To find out whether the public had an accurate estimate of the nation's 75 percent on-time high school graduation rate, we ask respondents to give their best estimate for the schools in their community.[20] The public estimates, on average, that 72 percent of students graduated within four years, just 3 percentage points below the actual level. Teacher estimates of the graduation rate at their local schools are slightly larger than the estimates of the public as a whole. They estimate the graduation rate to be 78 percent, 3 percentage points higher than the actual rate but once again within 3 percent of the true rate.

Information Matters Little

Given the modest underestimate of graduation rates, knowing the facts might be expected to have little effect on the public's evaluation of the nation's schools. To see whether that is the case, we told a random portion of respondents in 2009 the actual graduation rate but did not tell the other portion. The impact of being given the correct information on school evaluations is, as expected, only mildly positive, not large enough to be statistically significant.[21] Given the knowledge already available to the public, the provision of further information has negligible effects on public opinion.

Conclusions

That the public has modest amounts of information about many education policies is hardly surprising. Ordinary citizens prefer to spend their time on matters other than gathering detailed information about policy innovations, teacher salaries, or government expenditures. A general lack of knowledge—and even large, systematic underestimates of taxpayer costs—may merely be a way of life in a world where citizens must give first priority to doing their jobs, caring for their families, and solving their own financial problems. Most people may think that their free time is better spent on relaxation and entertainment than on fact-gathering in government documents or newspapers and magazines.

The information deficit is not simply a function of citizen inattention, however. Despite the emergence of school accountability programs, basic information about what schools do and how much they cost remains difficult to come by. For example, the total cost of K–12 education is obscured by the fact that education is financed by federal, state, and local levels of government. Although the share contributed by each level of government varies from one state to the next, in general local districts pony up about 45 percent of the total, state governments another 45 percent, and the federal government about 10 percent. Federal contributions flow through multiple channels that fund specific programs and activities, such as subsidized lunches, special education, compensatory education, vocational training, and many others. The exact way in which states support education varies across the country, but typically funds are distributed not only through all-purpose grants but also through a host of separate channels, including school construction aid, student transportation assistance, special education grants, and extra monies for small districts and those facing declining enrollments or charter school competition.[22]

The U.S. Department of Education does collate expenditures and revenues from all sources and releases that information periodically so that it is possible to obtain per-student expenditures for each school district. We used that valuable source of information to inform respondents during the course of the survey experiments reported earlier in this chapter. Nonetheless, that information becomes public only three or four years after the expenditure has taken place. As of June 2013, the most recent information on school expenditure available was for the 2008–09 school year.

When information is released only after considerable delay, it has little impact on public discourse. Journalists do not find outdated material newsworthy, and the facts are difficult to insert into political debates about what is needed currently. Every fact about school expenditures some years previously can be challenged on the grounds that the situation has changed in the meantime—the cost of living has risen, the number of students enrolled has changed, budget cuts have taken place, and so forth. Yet the dated material made available by the U.S. Department of Education is the only reliable source on total per-pupil expenditures for school districts. Neither districts themselves nor state governments make any effort to total the overall per-pupil cost of education in each school district.

Even so, information on per-pupil expenditures is more accessible than information on average teacher salaries. While the former becomes public knowledge after a delay of several years, the latter is virtually impossible to obtain. Some (but certainly not all) school districts post the teacher salary schedule on their websites, allowing the viewer to identify minimum and (sometimes) maximum salaries. But because the schedules do not identify the number of teachers within each category, the average salary in the district cannot be calculated. Nor do most states collect that information from the districts to which they give grants, despite the fact that state aid covers, on average, about as much of the total cost of education as do district sources. And despite the historic role of the federal government in the collection of key education statistics, it does not regularly collect and disseminate salary information by school district or state.[23] The only organizations that regularly provide salary information at the state level are the American Federation of Teachers and the National Education Association, organizations with strong vested interests in the topic. Neither provides information on the cost of the benefits—pensions, health care, disability insurance, life insurance, and so forth—that teachers receive. Only salary information, not total compensation, is available.

It is striking that public opinion is so much better informed about the outcomes of education, such as graduation rates, than about key inputs such as per-pupil expenditures and teacher salaries. While the former are undoubtedly more important, they also are affected by a host of non-governmental factors—family support, student commitment, peer pressure—over which policymakers have little direct control. But spending is a governmental act, a political act, an act that is presumably shaped by the opinions of the public at large. If the government leaves the public uninformed about matters that it is supposed to be directly influencing, political practice falls short of democratic ideals.

Iron triangles do not want the public to know how well they are treated by government, and they often discourage government from publicizing accurate information. In all likelihood, the lack of current information on teacher salaries and per-pupil expenditures is not a bureaucratic oversight but a response to pressure that the education iron triangle brings to bear on policymakers. Information corrodes. Iron retains its strength if kept safely from the open air.

But what happens when the public is informed about student performance in their local school district? Does that also change public opinion? Does that close—or does it further open—the division of opinion between teachers and the public? That is the topic for chapter 6.

CHAPTER SIX

Further Oxidization

JUST AS THE education iron triangle benefits from lack of transparency about school expenditures and teacher salaries, so too does it draw strength from the perception that local schools are performing at an acceptable level.[1] Americans do not have a false sense of complacency about the educational performance of the nation as a whole. They know that as many as one student in four fails to graduate from high school on the expected schedule. They also know that the performance of American students in key subjects like mathematics lags behind that of their peers in many other countries. When we ask respondents to rank the United States against other countries, the average estimate puts the United States in 19th place, not much above the official estimate provided by the Program for International Student Assessment (PISA), administered by the Organization for Economic Cooperation and Development, which puts the United States somewhere between 22nd and 28th place among the countries it surveyed.

Yet we have also shown (in chapter 4) that Americans tend to assign far higher grades to the public schools in their own community than to those of the nation. One potential explanation for this paradox is that despite having a solid understanding of the overall level of performance in the nation as a whole, Americans are misinformed about where their local schools rank within the national performance distribution. They may simply be unwilling to admit that the schools in their own community do not prepare students adequately for college or a career. Or perhaps they lack access to sources of information that would allow them to make an informed judgment on the matter, allowing hope to triumph over reality. The latter possibility deserves to be taken seriously.

Across all 50 states, schools operate under accountability programs that require districts to provide information to the public about the share of students who achieve at proficient levels on standardized tests in the core academic subjects of reading and math. Under the federal No Child Left Behind Act, however, each state is free to set its own proficiency standards. Many have set relatively low standards; few have set the bar high. In 2011, for example, Alabama reported that 77 percent of its eighth-grade students were proficient in math based on their performance on its state test. The same year, just 20 percent of Alabama's eighth-graders met the standard of math proficiency set by the U.S. Department of Education's National Assessment of Educational Progress (NAEP). In other words, Alabama deemed many more of its students to be proficient than did NAEP. U.S. Secretary of Education Arne Duncan has gone so far as to accuse states like Alabama of "lying to children and parents" by setting low expectations for student performance.[2] And it is easy to imagine how the lenient standards that many states have adopted could encourage citizens to evaluate their schools more generously—or at least allow such generous evaluations to persist unchecked.

All of that could change with the advent of the Common Core State Standards (CCSS), an initiative of the National Governors Association and the Council of Chief State School Officers through which forty-six states have committed to adopt a common and more demanding set of expectations for student performance. Some education observers believe that CCSS will finally clarify for students, parents, and educators what high school graduates need to learn if they are to be prepared for college or a career. Others believe that CCSS interferes with local control of schools, limits teacher creativity, and diverts classroom time and energy from instruction to test preparation. While the teacher unions have officially endorsed the initiative, rank-and-file members have increasingly expressed displeasure with the changes. But as pundits and practitioners thrust and parry over these issues, they may be overlooking CCSS's potential impact on public perceptions of school quality and public support for school reforms.

If CCSS is fully implemented as proposed by its most ardent adherents, it can be expected to alter the information that Americans have about student performance in their local schools. Currently, the public has no national metric to guide its assessment of local school performance. At best, they can find out the percentage of students who are proficient according to state tests, which are typically undemanding. Were a common metric used to assess student performance, as CCSS promises, each school district could be ranked nationally as well as within its state. In addition, the common standards would be higher standards for virtually all districts nationwide. If students fall short of this higher benchmark, the public in the districts will see levels of performance that are worse than those to which they are accustomed.

Recently, the state of New York adopted a much higher definition of proficiency in anticipation of full implementation of CCSS in its schools. When the new test results were released, the percentage of students identified as proficient in math dropped from 65 percent to 31 percent and in English from 55 percent to 31 percent. The gap between white and minority students widened, as only 16 percent of black students and 18 percent of Hispanic students were deemed proficient in English. The results ignited a debate in New York City's heated mayoral campaign, in which candidates searched for ways to distinguish themselves from the outgoing administration of Mayor Michael Bloomberg. Asked for his opinion, Secretary Duncan replied that "the only way you improve is to tell the truth. And sometimes that's a brutal truth."[3]

Such truth-telling promises to become a regular occurrence as the CCSS rollout proceeds—and it will no doubt come as a shock to many Americans accustomed to more reassuring signals about the performance of students in their local schools. What is unknown—and of considerable interest for our purposes in this book—is how being told the truth about local student performance will affect public opinion. Is there reason to think that rigorous national standards, with accompanying measures of student performance, will alter public opinion on education issues? If so, will teachers agree? Or will any change of opinion further widen the gaps that exist between them and the rest of the public? To shed light on this issue, we draw on results from an additional survey experiment conducted in 2013.

Our findings reveal that when respondents learn how their local schools rank in comparison with the performance of schools elsewhere in the state or the nation as a whole, they become more supportive of school choice proposals, such as making school vouchers available to all families; expanding charter schools; and giving parents the power to trigger changes in their local school. Opinion changes on other policy questions are also identified.

These shifts in public opinion are generally larger for those respondents living in districts with below-average national rankings. On learning the rankings of their local public schools, Americans also give them lower evaluations, just as they express less confidence in and support for teachers.

Teachers, in turn, also lower their evaluations of local public schools when provided with information about their state or national rank. Yet their opinions on policy matters are, by and large, unchanged. As a consequence, we conclude that the advent of common standards has the potential to deepen the divide between the American public and teachers.

Survey Methodology

The experiment generating these results was conducted as part of our 2013 survey. To carry out the experiment, we divided respondents randomly into groups of roughly 1,000. One representative group was left *uninformed* about the performance of students in its local schools.[4] Two additional groups were given specific information about the performance of students in the local public schools deemed relevant for gauging the possible effects of the Common Core on public opinion. In particular, these two groups were told either the state ranking of the average student in each respondent's district on standardized tests of achievement or the national ranking of the performance of the average student in the district. The differences between the opinions of the uninformed group and those of each of these two groups provide direct estimates of the impact of new information about student performance on public assessments of local schools and public views about school reform policies. Once the information on state and national rankings is introduced, respondents could review that information throughout the remainder of the survey by clicking on a link provided on each page, allowing respondents to make use of the data while contemplating their evaluations of schools and considering their views on policy matters. Thus all policy questions are explicitly subjected to the treatment information.

How Information on Local District Ranking Changes Public Opinion

We expect new information about local district rankings to alter public opinion in four domains. If the new information surprises respondents by indicating that the district is doing less well than previously thought, the public, on learning the truth of the matter, is likely to

—lower its evaluation of local schools

—become more supportive of educational alternatives for families

—alter its thinking about current policies affecting teacher compensation and retention

—reassess its thinking about school and student accountability policies.

In this regard, we expect the largest changes to occur in those districts that rank below the median district nationwide. Meanwhile, should local schools perform better than expected, as they may for at least some respondents living in districts in the upper half of the national rankings, then just the opposite pattern of results may emerge.

However, we expect little movement in response to this information for teachers, who have more familiarity with how students are performing and less incentive to update their opinions on policies that would cut against their economic interest. Therefore, we expect the provision of new information on performance to widen gaps between them and the public.

Evaluations of Schools

Uninformed members of the public give much more positive assessments when asked to evaluate the schools in their local community than they offer when asked about the nation's schools (see chapter 4). Overall, 50 percent say that their local public schools deserve an "A" or a "B" on the scale traditionally used to evaluate students, but only 21 percent say so when respondents are asked about schools nationwide. The distance between these two judgments narrows, however, when respondents are told the ranking of their local school district either within their state or the nation as a whole. The share of those giving local schools one of the two highest grades drops from 50 percent among the uninformed to just 44 percent among those told the district's ranking relative to other districts across the state (see figure 6-1). When given the district's national ranking, the share giving an "A" or "B" grade drops to 41 percent. Interestingly, the estimated decline is roughly the same regardless of whether the respondent lives in a school district ranking above or below the national average. That suggests that Americans' perceptions about where their local schools rank in the national performance distribution may be inflated across the board, not just in low-performing school districts.

Figure 6-1. *Percentage of General Public and Teachers Giving an "A" or a "B" Grade to Local Schools, 2013*

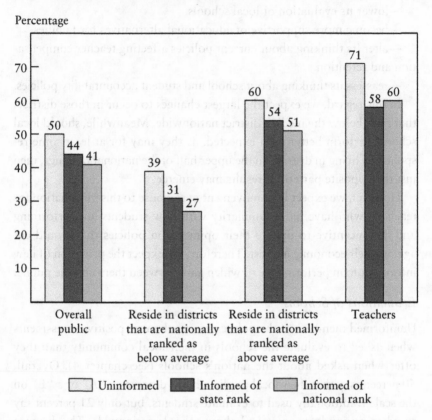

Percentage

| | Uninformed | Informed of state rank | Informed of national rank |

   Table 6-1 presents similar results for both informed and uninformed members of both the public and the teaching force on multiple topics. In table 6-2 the same results are broken out for members of the public by the national ranking of the school district in which the respondent lived. The remainder of the chapter highlights the key results presented in these tables. Note, for example, the finding reported in the second row of table 6-1 for the impact of information about district ranking on the public's evaluations of the nation's schools. In contrast to its large impact on evaluations of local schools, this information has virtually no impact on evaluations of the nation's schools. Only 21 percent of the uninformed members of the public think that the nation's schools deserve an "A" or a "B," and only 20 percent of those informed of their local district's rank-ing hold that view of the nation's schools.

That should not surprise given that the provided information concerns the ranking of the respondent's own local school district rather than the nation's schools as a whole. Moreover, as noted above, the public already has a pretty good understanding of the quality of the nation's schools. Americans are clear-headed—even somewhat skeptical—about the nation's schools. As a consequence, the new information does not alter their per-ceptions of schools across the country.

Taken together, these results provide a partial resolution of the appar-ent paradox generated by the public's skeptical assessments of the nation's schools and the much more favorable ratings given to schools in their own community. The size of the differential in the share awarding an "A" or "B" drops from 29 percentage points to 21 percentage points once information about national ranking is supplied. In other words, the sup-posed paradox attenuates once some basic information is supplied about the performance of local public schools.

School Choice

As can also be seen in table 6-1, information about local district rankings also shifts the public's views about school choice programs—including charter schools, parent trigger mechanisms, and especially school vouch-ers—generally increasing support.

VOUCHERS

It is sometimes thought by school choice advocates that *targeted* school vouchers—that is, vouchers limited to students from low-income fami-lies—have more public support than do *universal* voucher programs, which allow any family to make use of a government voucher to attend a private school. Accordingly, the school voucher programs enacted by leg-islatures in Wisconsin, Ohio, Indiana, and Washington, D.C., have all targeted students from low-income families. But we find that support for universal vouchers expands when the public learns about the relative ranking of their local district schools, while support for targeted school vouchers actually declines somewhat.

Overall, 54 percent of the uninformed public respondents support "a [universal voucher] proposal that would give families with children in

Table 6-1. *Impact of Performance Information on Opinion of the General Public and Teachers, 2013*[a]

Percent

	General public			Teachers		
Issue/opinion	Uninformed	Informed of national rank	Informed of state rank	Uninformed	Informed of national rank	Informed of state rank
Grades assigned to schools						
Give A or B to local schools	50	41**	44**	71	60**	58**
Give A or B to nation's schools	21	20	20	36	33	34
School choice						
Expand choice with universal vouchers	54	71**	66**	41	34	43
Use government funds for means-tested vouchers	48	41*	45	33	16**	24
Allow charter schools	68	72*	70	46	42	50
Support parent trigger	66	68	69	40	36	44
Teacher policy						
Have confidence in teachers	40	39	36*	77	75	77
Teacher unions are harmful	58	56	58	36	27	38
Eliminate tenure	60	70**	66**	38	36	41
Increase teacher pay (no salary information)	54	57	62**	79	86	79
Increase teacher pay (with salary information)	37	33	35	63	74	72
Accountability						
Support Common Core State Standards	83	81	82	87	79	72**
Use test for grade promotion	85	83	86	68	80**	68
Require graduation test	84	79**	82	81	70**	72**

a. See appendix B for the wording of the questions.

* (**) Difference with uninformed opinion is statistically significant at the 0.1 (0.05) level.

Table 6-2. *Impact of Performance Information on Opinion of the General Public, by District Performance, 2013*[a]

Percent

Issue/opinion	Reside in districts that are ranked below the median nationally			Reside in districts that are ranked above the median nationally		
	Uninformed	Informed of national rank	Informed of state rank	Uninformed	Informed of national rank	Informed of state rank
Grades assigned to schools						
Give A or B to local schools	39	27**	31*	60	51**	54**
Give A or B to nation's schools	21	19	19	20	17	17
School choice						
Expand choice with universal vouchers	59	79**	76**	50	64**	59*
Use government funds for means-tested vouchers	53	51	42**	44	33*	48
Allow charter schools	66	73**	78**	69	71	63
Support parent trigger	62	72**	69*	69	65	69
Teacher policy						
Have confidence in teachers	40	32**	33**	40	44	38
Teacher unions are harmful	49	53	57**	66	58**	58*
Eliminate tenure	54	70**	61*	65	70	70
Increase teacher pay (no salary information)	61	61	63	49	54	62**
Increase teacher pay (with salary information)	41	29**	37	32	36	34
Accountability						
Support Common Core State Standards	84	80	84	83	81	80
Use test for grade promotion	86	85	89	84	82	84
Require graduation test	82	77*	87**	86	81*	79**

a. See appendix B for the wording of the questions.

*(**) Difference with uninformed opinion is statistically significant at the 0.1 (0.05) level.

public schools a wider choice by allowing them to enroll their children in private schools instead, with government helping to pay the tuition."[5] Support for universal vouchers increases from 54 percent to 71 percent when respondents are told how students in their local district ranked nationally and to 66 percent when the state ranking is provided. In districts that perform in the bottom half of the test score distribution, support for vouchers climbs even higher, to 79 percent, when information is supplied. In short, information about student performance dramatically increases public support for universal vouchers.

Not so, though, when the public is asked about a proposal "that would use government funds to pay the tuition of low-income students who choose to attend private schools." Such a targeted voucher proposal leaves uninformed Americans evenly divided between support and opposition, with 48 percent in favor. When respondents are told how well local students rank nationally, however, support for targeted voucher programs falls to 41 percent.

Respondents in lower-performing districts who are told of their district's national ranking respond to the targeted voucher proposal no differently than those left uninformed. But when respondents are told of their district's state ranking, support for targeted vouchers falls by 9 percentage points. The opposite pattern was found for respondents in higher-performing districts. Information about their district's ranking within their state does not change their opinion about targeted vouchers. But when told about their district's national ranking, their support for targeted vouchers falls by 11 percentage points. Apparently, learning about their district's national ranking shocks those living in above-average districts even when learning about their district's state ranking does not.

In sum, 71 percent of those informed of their local district's national ranking favor universal vouchers, but only 41 percent support targeted vouchers. That differs sharply from the 54 percent and 48 percent support for universal and targeted vouchers, respectively, among those not provided that information. What is a statistically insignificant 6 percentage-point difference between targeted and universal vouchers widens to a dramatic 30 percentage-point difference when basic information about school rankings is supplied.

Why should learning about a local district ranking sharply increase support for universal vouchers but have the opposite impact on support for targeted vouchers? The most plausible explanation is that the public is shocked at the low ranking of their district and, in response, exhibits greater support for alternatives to the traditional public school. Such alternatives, however, should be open to all families, not just those with low incomes. Having learned that school quality in their district is lower than previously thought, the public endorses a policy solution that reaches beyond the particular problems of low-income families.

CHARTERS

New information also affects public opinion about charter schools. Among uninformed respondents, 68 percent "support the formation of charter schools." When they are given the national ranking of local district schools, charter support shifts upward to 72 percent. Respondents in below-average districts are particularly likely to back charters when informed about their school's state and national rankings: their support for charter schools jumps by 12 percentage points and 7 percentage points when they learn about their state and national rankings, respectively. Meanwhile, the opinion of respondents in districts whose national ranking is above average does not change in response to information about district ranking.

PARENT TRIGGER

A similar pattern appears for a proposal that has come to be known as the "parent trigger," which would allow a majority of parents whose children attend a low-performing traditional public school "to sign a petition requiring the district to convert the school into a charter." Overall, providing information about state or national rankings causes no shift in the support of the general public for this idea. However, a large effect occurs among those living in districts that have below-average rankings. In those districts, support jumps from 62 percent to 69 percent when respondents are informed of their district's performance relative to that of other districts within the state and to 72 percent when they are informed of its performance relative to that of other districts nationwide. Again, those living in districts with above-average ranking do not alter their opinion with respect to the parent trigger when given information.

Overall, public support for school choice increases when the public is informed of their local district's ranking in the state or nation. The jump in support is particularly large among those residing in districts that have a below-average ranking. Just as information on state and national ranking lowers evaluations of the public schools, it increases the willingness of the public to support alternatives to the traditional public school. When it comes to vouchers, however, the upward shift is conditional on school choice being provided for all students, not just those from low-income families.

Teachers and Teacher Policy

Information about local district rankings not only alters public readiness to consider educational alternatives but also changes opinion on teacher quality, teacher unions, teacher tenure, and teacher compensation.

EVALUATING TEACHERS

Uninformed respondents' tepid evaluation of the nation's schools carries over to their assessments of public school teachers. Only 40 percent say that they have either "a lot" or "complete" trust and confidence in public school teachers. Meanwhile, 59 percent say that they have only a "little" or "some" trust and confidence in public school teachers. Overall, information about state and national rankings does not alter those assessments. But the level of trust and confidence in teachers falls by 7 and 8 percentage points in below-average districts when respondents are told about state and national rankings, respectively. No statistically significant impacts are observed in the districts with above-average rankings.

TEACHER UNIONS

Fifty-eight percent of the uninformed public report that teacher unions have "a generally negative effect" on public schools. Interestingly, though, uninformed respondents from districts with below-average rankings express much more favorable views of teacher unions: just 49 percent have a negative view of unions, while no less than 66 percent of those in districts with above-average rankings do.

When respondents are informed about district rankings, their opinions about teacher unions shift in opposite directions. In below-average districts, negative evaluations of unions rise from 49 percent to 57 percent when state ranking information is supplied, while in above-average districts, negative assessments shift downward, from 66 percent to 58 per cent. A similar but less dramatic turnaround is observed when national ranking information is supplied. In other words, informing people of the ranking of their local school district changes the public's views of teacher unions—but the shift in opinion depends on whether the local district has a high or low ranking relative to that of other districts.

TEACHER TENURE

Information about local school rankings also strengthens the public's opposition to teacher job protections. Sixty percent of the uninformed public favors elimination of tenure. When respondents are told how their local schools rank in the state and the country, opposition to tenure for teachers rises further, growing by 6 and 10 percentage points, respectively. The difference between the informed and the uninformed in below-average districts is slightly larger—7 percentage points when respondents are given the state ranking and 16 percentage points when given the national ranking.

TEACHER COMPENSATION

When it comes to teacher pay, the influence of information is more complex. Among uninformed respondents, 54 percent of the non-teaching public favors a salary increase. That percentage climbs to 62 percent when they are told the state ranking of their local school and to 57 percent when they are told the national ranking (the latter change is not statistically significant). As in previous years, the public in 2013 appears perfectly willing to pay teachers more in order to address the poorer-than-expected quality of local schools.

As it turns out, though, that conclusion is not altogether warranted. When the public is informed about current teacher salary levels, its enthusiasm for salary increases wanes. Instead of the 54 percent of uninformed respondents who are in favor, only 37 percent of those informed of current pay levels endorse salary increases. A further downward shift in support—to 29 percent—occurs among respondents residing in school districts ranking below the national average when respondents are given both salary and ranking information. Among those living in above-average districts, however, support for raising teacher salaries remains essentially unchanged when they learn of their district's national standing.

In other words, public views on teacher compensation are influenced both by information on current levels of spending and by information on a local district's national ranking. Information on current spending reduces public support for increased expenditures in all districts, and support for salary increases drops further in below-average districts when respondents are informed of both current salaries and their district ranking. In the absence of salary information, however, support for salary increases climbs in districts that rank above average provided that respondents are told of that ranking.

Taken as a whole, information about local school rankings has a less substantial impact on public thinking about teacher policy than it has on school choice policies. Whereas the impacts on school choice were large and consistent (with the notable exception of targeted school vouchers), the impacts on teacher policy depend more on the district's national ranking. Informed respondents told that they live in below-average districts are more likely to lower their assessment of teacher quality, withdraw their support for teacher unions, become more opposed to teacher tenure, and become more reluctant to back salary increases for teachers. Respondents told that they live in above-average districts, however, actually back higher salaries for teachers (if they are not informed of current levels) and give greater support to teacher unions.

Accountability

Having seen the lower proficiency ratings that students received with CCSS, critics in New York are already calling for the elimination of the new standards and testing. As one New York City principal (and former CCSS backer) recently wrote in the *Washington Post*,

> It will be parents who insist that school not be a place of the continual measurement of deficits, instead standing as places that allow students to show what they know beyond a standardized test. Parents won't "buy the bunk" and they will tire of data driven, rather than student driven, instruction.[6]

We find little evidence for such a backlash against Common Core and test-based accountability. In the absence of any information about local student performance, 83 percent of Americans support CCSS. Information about state or national ranking makes no discernible impact.

We also asked respondents what they think about requiring third-grade students to pass a state reading test before moving to the fourth grade. More than four in five uninformed respondents support that requirement, and information about local district ranking does not reduce support for this sort of high-stakes testing in either above-average or below-average districts. However, that information does have a slight effect on support for high school graduation exams. As with high-stakes tests for third-graders, Americans come out strongly in favor of graduation require-ments. In both high- and low-performing districts, however, support for that requirement drops 5 percentage points when respondents are in-formed of how students in their community compare with those in the rest of the nation. Even then, however, roughly 80 percent of respondents ex-press support for graduation requirements.

In short, there is scant evidence that better information about a dis-trict's ranking weakens support for accountability. Any downward shift is limited to one item, and it is modest relative to the overall sup-port for these policies and evident only among residents of below-average districts.

How Information on Local District Ranking Changes Teacher Opinion

To the extent that teachers are better informed about student performance or more committed to their policy views, the provision of new informa-tion about their local school district's state or national rank should have a smaller impact on their views. For the most part, this is indeed what we observe.

Evaluations of Schools

The grades assigned to local schools are an exception to this overall pat-tern, however. Although teachers tend to give higher evaluations to both local schools and schools across the country than does the public, they respond to information about school quality in similar ways. The share of teachers giving local schools one of the two highest grades drops from 71 percent among the uninformed to 60 percent among those told the district's national ranking and 58 percent among those told the district's state ranking (see figure 6-1).

School Choice

Information about local district rankings shifts upward public support for school choice programs—including charter schools, parent trigger mechanisms, and especially universal school vouchers. Teachers are not swayed in the same way. For example, information increases support for universal vouchers among the general public, but it has no effect on teacher opinions. Nor do the opinions of teachers about charter schools or the parent trigger proposal change when information on district ranking is provided. Information comparing their local school district with those in the rest of the nation reduces support for targeted vouchers, however. Without that information, 33 percent of teachers support targeted vouchers; with it, only 16 percent do.

In no case, then, do teachers become more supportive of choice. Generally, information about student performance in local schools widens the opinion gap between teachers and the rest of the public, especially those living in below-average districts. For example, the 13-percentage-point gap in support for universal vouchers between uninformed teachers and nonteachers nearly triples in the presence of information comparing local schools with those in the rest of the nation. The gap between teachers and members of the general public who live in the lowest-performing districts grows even wider, to 45 percentage points. Similar patterns hold for opinion on charter schools and parent trigger laws.

Teachers and Teacher Policy

The provision of information on district rank has little impact on teachers' views regarding their peers and the policies that govern their work lives. Teachers, unsurprisingly, have more confidence in public school teachers than does the rest of the public. Seventy-seven percent of them report "a lot" or "complete" confidence—a number that hardly budges when teachers are told about the state or national rankings of their local district schools. Teachers are also just as positive about unions when told how their local schools compare with the rest of the state as when they are given no additional information.

On the issue of teacher tenure, teachers again remain unmoved. Only 38 percent favor elimination of job protections when given no information about local school performance, and roughly the same small share favor tenure elimination when information on district ranking is supplied. And teacher opinion appears equally impervious to information about district performance when it comes to their compensation.

Accountability

Even though the general public's endorsement of the CCSS is unaffected by information on district ranking, teachers respond with greater negativity toward CCSS when told how local schools compare with others across the state. Without information, 87 percent of teachers support CCSS, a figure that drops by 15 percentage points when they are given that information. Thus, the pattern observed in other policy areas reverses when it comes to CCSS. On the topics of choice and teacher policy, teachers were generally less sensitive to new information than the public. Here, teachers are far more sensitive.

Teacher opinion on other accountability policies is more puzzling. Teachers are less favorable than the rest of the public toward requiring third-graders to pass a reading exam before being promoted to the next grade, but they are still generally supportive of that requirement. Among teachers who are not provided information about state or national rankings, 68 percent support the testing requirement. Teachers do respond to the national rankings, but not in the way that many would suspect. Teachers actually become more supportive of the testing requirement, by 12 percentage points— almost eliminating any gap between them and non-teachers. For graduation tests, uninformed teachers are nearly identical to the rest of the public: 84 percent and 81 percent, respectively, support requiring the tests. Both groups respond to information about school quality by backing off their support for the tests, but the magnitude of the shift differs. Whereas non-teacher support for graduation tests drops by 5 percentage points when non-teachers are told how their local districts compare with the rest of the country, teacher support drops by more than twice as much when teachers are told. Both groups remain supportive of the testing requirement, but it is worth noting that the gap between them widens.

Common Core and Public Opinion

If CCSS enhances public knowledge of the performance of local schools relative to that of schools elsewhere in the state and nation, the iron triangle may begin to rust, especially (but not exclusively) in lower-performing school districts. Public assessments of local schools would shift in a more skeptical direction; support for universal voucher initiatives, charter schools, and the parent trigger mechanism would increase; limits to teacher tenure would gain greater public support; and both teacher unions and demands for increases in teacher salaries would confront greater public skepticism. In nearly every case, however, the shift in opinion is confined to non-teachers. In other words, CCSS has the potential to further isolate teachers from the rest of the public.

These conclusions, however, come with caveats. When information is supplied as part of a survey, it is not subject to contestation by those who have an interest in obfuscating certain facts and emphasizing others. Further, our findings do not touch on the substantive merits of the CCSS-based curriculum that is the focus of so much public discussion. And perhaps most consequentially, a long stride separates changes in public opinion and political action. It would take considerable leadership and political mobilization to capitalize on any changes in public opinion that CCSS might arouse.

CHAPTER SEVEN
Divisions Within

Two years before Rahm Emmanuel's reform proposals provoked a teacher strike in Chicago, New York City (NYC) mayor Michael Bloomberg announced his plans for "ending tenure as we know it." The NYC school system had come under fire for granting tenure to teachers without adequate assessment of their competence. Awarded at the end of three years of teaching, tenure made it extremely difficult for school administrators to fire low-performing teachers and eventually gave rise to the school system's notorious "rubber room" for warehousing egregiously incompetent teachers who nonetheless continued to draw their salaries. After a more stringent performance assessment process was introduced, NYC schools granted tenure to 58 percent of eligible teachers, a steep drop from the 97 percent who typically had received it in earlier years. When a local public radio station featured a story on the new tenure rate, teachers and former teachers flooded the telephone lines. Unsurprisingly, most callers lambasted moves to tighten tenure requirements. But a few teachers criticized the proposals as too weak. Said one teacher, who left the Bronx to take a job in Westchester County, "It is way too easy for teachers in NYC to get tenure. You only have to show up for three years, and you're basically granted it. . . . I was among really bad teachers, and they got it just because it was three years."[1]

Not all teachers think alike, despite the unified teacher voice heard through many a news outlet. "Are Teachers the Problem?" headlined a *Time* magazine story on teacher backlash against school reform.[2] Nor is it only union critics who portray teachers as a monolithic bloc. When New Jersey governor Chris Christie attempted to draw a distinction between most Garden State teachers and union activists who opposed him, one activist replied, "The teachers are the unions. We are the same people."[3]

Yet enough teachers dissent from union positions that it has proven possible to form alternative, reform-minded teacher organizations. Two NYC teachers, disgruntled with the school board's and the union's disregard for their input, launched Educators 4 Excellence (E4E), a group that committed its members to a stringent reform platform. According to journalist Richard Lee Colvin, "Teachers who want to join are expected to pledge to support using value-added test-score data in evaluations, higher hurdles to achieving tenure, the elimination of seniority-driven layoffs, school choice, and merit pay."[4] Outside NYC, the group opened chapters in Los Angeles and Minnesota. Other organizations—Teach Plus, the Hope Street Group, and the New Millennium Initiative, to name a few—are recruiting teachers for advocacy work independent of teacher unions. Still other reform-minded caucuses are forming within existing organizations. For example, Colvin describes a faction within the United Teachers of Los Angeles (UTLA), known as NewTLA:

> In November of 2011, the NewTLA caucus got 85 of its members elected to the 350-member union House of Representatives and helped elect a candidate for president of the union who was thought to be more amenable to reforms. Soon after, the union agreed to grant individual schools flexibility over the school calendar, hiring, and assignment of teachers. Then [in February 2012], the caucus supported asking UTLA's membership to direct the union to negotiate with the district on the creation of a new teacher-evaluation system. The measure won easily.[5]

Do these groups represent only a minuscule sliver of the teaching profession, or do they reflect deeper divisions? Do they reflect the views of younger teachers, who will be the teaching force of the future? Are they representative of a substantial conservative faction within the teaching profession, including many who identify with the Republican Party? What other social cleavages are contributing to internal divisions? Are they so large and deep that they belie the presumed unity and singularity of the profession?

In the not-too-distant past, teachers were divided into two rival organizations, the National Education Association (NEA) and the American Federation of Teachers (AFT). The NEA, the larger of the organizations, was originally led by school superintendents, and it claimed to speak on behalf of the entire education community. The more militant AFT focused specifically on better salaries and working conditions for classroom teachers. When Al Shanker and his AFT colleagues called for a strike in New York City in 1960, the local chapter of the NEA refused to participate on the grounds that the strike was in violation of the law. Only after the AFT began to recruit teachers away from the NEA did the latter organization elect a more aggressive leadership and endorse collective bargaining in the districts where it commanded a majority of the teachers. To this day, NEA remains more popular in the South and among teachers in small town, suburban, and rural districts, while the AFT's membership is concentrated in urban areas of the Northeast and Midwest.

Although the two organizations have agreed not to raid one another's membership and have cooperated in the electoral sphere, efforts to unite the two organizations have failed to win a majority vote of the members of either organization. The continuing division between NEA and AFT is a reminder that teachers across the United States form a diverse group of people who hold varying opinions on many matters. Are there underlying differences in teacher opinion that could widen the gap between two entities that were until recently organizational rivals? Could one of them be transformed into an agent for school reform?

In this chapter we consider the potential for the development of a new, politically significant split within the teaching profession. In doing so, we offer little reason for optimism among those who hope that support for school reform will soon emerge. Although we find cleavages among teachers that parallel those in the public at large, the internal divisions are marginal, not fundamental, and they take shapes that are quite different from the ones preferred by reformers. Younger teachers defend their prerogatives with as much militancy as older ones. Cultural divides can be identified within the teaching profession, but they tend to disappear on issues that touch on teacher prerogatives. The views of black and Hispanic teachers seem to differ from those of white teachers, but the sample of minority teachers is too small for us to estimate these differences precisely. But before presenting the available evidence on these matters, we need first to describe the social composition of today's teaching force and offer a couple of methodological caveats.

Who Are the Teachers?

The average teacher is very different from the average American adult (see table 7-1). First, the teaching force, obviously enough, is better educated.[6] Teachers enjoy a higher income than the general public: the median household income of teachers is $15,000 higher than the median household income of the general public. A relatively small percentage of teachers come from a minority background. Only 6 percent identify themselves as Hispanic, and just 8 percent say that they are African American; for the public as a whole, those percentages are 15 percent and 12 percent, respectively.

Teachers differ from the general public in other ways as well. No less than 73 percent are women, a reminder that the stereotypical image of a teacher as "schoolmarm" is more than a lingering misperception. Thirty percent of teachers but only 23 percent of the general public have a school-age child themselves. The percentage of teachers who own their homes (84 percent) is higher than that of the general public (74 percent), as is the percentage who send their children to private school. The teachers in our sample as a whole are slightly younger than the general population. That makes sense given that our measure of "teacher" captures current employment and thereby excludes retirees.

Teachers are considerably less culturally and politically distinctive than they often are portrayed in the popular press. No less than 35 percent of teachers indicate an evangelical Protestant religious identity by saying that they have been "born again," a percentage not much different from the 39 percent of the public that give a similar reply. Teachers also are politically diverse, despite appearances conveyed by the close association of teacher unions with the Democratic Party. The share of Republicans among teachers (31 percent) exceeds the share of Republicans among the general population (24 percent). Meanwhile, 39 percent of teachers in our sample identify themselves as Democrats, a figure only slightly higher than that for the general population. The remaining teachers identify themselves as independent or give some other affiliation.

Table 7-1. *Background Characteristics of General Public and Teachers,*
2011

Percent, unless otherwise shown

Characteristic	General public[a]	Teachers
Race/ethnicity		
White	66	79
Black	12	8
Hispanic	15	6
Education		
Less than high school	14	1
High school only	31	4
Some college	29	9
College or higher	26	86
Median household income category	$50,000–$59,999	$75,000–$84,999
Age[b]		
Average age	46	44
Youngest group (18–41)	41	37
Middle group (42–55)	27	35
Oldest group (56+)	32	27
Own home	72	84
Parent	23	30
Female	51	73
"Born again" Christian	39	35
Partisanship		
Democrat	35	39
Independent	41	30
Republican	24	31
Children in private school (K–12)[c]	7	15

a. "General public" refers to the share of the sample that did not include public school teachers.

b. Groups were calculated based on thirds of the unweighted total sample; the percentages in each age group among the general public are not equivalent to thirds because these descriptive data are computed using post-stratification weights (see appendix A for further details on survey weights).

c. Among parents only.

In sum, our findings show that teachers are not a representative cross-section of the U.S. population. But neither are they an exploited underclass or a unified force of liberal, secular Democrats. Remaining to be explored is the political significance of the variation in the social, cultural, and political backgrounds of the members of the teaching profession.

Methodological Caveat

We cannot explore the political significance of the social, cultural, and political differences among teachers as thoroughly as we would like because only 436 public school teachers participated in our 2011 survey. (For the public as a whole, the sample consists of 2,183 respondents.)[7] Although both sets of respondents are representative of their respective national populations, the smaller number of teachers reduces the likelihood of our identifying statistically significant results when we explore internal divisions. Four hundred observations are quite sufficient if one wishes to compare the overall views of the teaching force with those of the public at large (as we did in chapter 2), but those numbers are less adequate for identifying differences between various types of teachers. Analyzing differences is especially challenging when the percentages of teachers in each category are not evenly balanced. When the composition of the teaching force is overwhelmingly white, it is difficult to collect enough information to identify accurately the differences between whites and the thirty-three African American teachers and twenty-eight Hispanic teachers in our 2011 survey. For that reason we do not report divisions of opinion along ethnic lines within the teaching force, as any estimate is made with considerable error. Even for the other divides, estimates are less precise because observations are fewer, and we may have failed to detect divisions within the teaching force even if they are fairly large.

To illustrate the significance of our varied sample sizes, appendix tables A-1 and A-2 display social cleavages within the general public and the teaching force, respectively. The stars identify statistically significant differences, and bolded numbers indicate situations in which a statistically significant difference places two majorities in opposition to one another. As is obvious to the naked eye, there are many more stars in table A-1 on the general public (seventy-seven, to be precise) than in table A-2 on teachers (forty-one). Ordinarily that kind of stargazing would correctly capture an overall message—that divisions are larger in the first table than in the second.

One cannot leap to that conclusion in this instance, however. Because a larger number of observations makes it more probable that divisions within the general public will be identified as statistically significant, it is easier for those divisions to "earn a star" than it is for similar divisions within the teaching force. Because we have more observations for the general public, we can ordinarily detect cleavages that are as small as 5 percentage points, but we cannot declare statistically significant differences between groups of teachers that are as large as 17 percentage points. If one counts up the number of observations in which the percentage-point differences are in double digits, one finds just about as many big differences within the teaching force as within the public at large. From that perspective, the extent of internal division appears to be roughly the same for the two populations.[8]

We draw two conclusions from these methodological considerations: First, the social cleavages within the teaching profession appear to be roughly similar in size and scope to those within the public at large. In other words, the teaching force is not so unified that teacher unions can count on unified backing across the board. Second, the nature of the divides within the teaching profession is more important than their sheer quantity. One must dig deeper to see what divisions might be politically relevant for the future of the education iron triangle. Of all the teacher divides, the most intriguing are those between younger and older teachers, between "born again" and other teachers, and between Democratic and Republican teachers.[9]

Younger versus Older Teachers

Perhaps the most important potential divide is that between younger and older teachers. If younger teachers hold distinctive views, the teaching profession may be undergoing significant change from within. In recent years, policy innovations have sought to identify and recruit new, change-oriented young people into the profession. Many states now offer alternative pathways to teaching that do not require prior completion of state-required education courses. Many charter schools and several big-city school districts are recruiting new staff members through Teach for

America, a reform-minded organization that seeks to recruit highly motivated teachers from selective colleges and universities. Teach Plus, a
Boston-based nonprofit organization that seeks to incorporate teachers'
voices into the policymaking process, published results of a nonrepresen-
tative online survey indicating that teachers with fewer than 10 years of
experience tend to support paying teachers on the basis of their performance, redesigning their retirement benefits, and evaluating them on the
basis of gains in student achievement—even as their more experienced
colleagues remain skeptical of those proposals. The group's leader, Celine
Coggins, says that "a new generation of teachers" is ready for reform because it "has been exposed to the magnitude of the achievement gap"
that now "motivates the commitment to teaching for so many."[10]

When we compare the views of the youngest third of teachers to the
oldest third, we discern significant differences of opinion between the
two. But our results do not support the most optimistic claims of those
who expect to see a reformed teaching force. The junior third of the
teaching force is no more in favor of implementing performance pay,
revising tenure policy, allowing principals to hire teachers without a state
teaching license, imposing stricter accountability requirements, or giving
families more school choice than older teachers. The younger teachers are
10 percentage points more likely to think that teacher unions do more
good than harm, although that difference is not statistically significant.
When junior teachers take a stand that differed from that of their seniors,
they often are more supportive of positions advocated by union leaders.
For example, younger teachers are more likely to support higher salaries,
to want to raise taxes to pay for more school spending, and to oppose
paying a higher share of teacher benefits out of their salaries. They are
also in favor of mainstreaming students and of qualifying the principal's
authority on disciplinary matters.

Some of those results are quite understandable. Current salaries and
benefit packages are weighted heavily in favor of senior teachers, and so
it only makes sense that their junior colleagues feel poorly compensated.
But if junior teachers do emerge as a counterforce to the current union
agenda, it is more likely to be for the purpose of promoting causes such
as those propounded by Karen Lewis in Chicago than the reform platform
offered by Educators 4 Excellence in New York City.[11]

Cultural Cleavages

Possibly more consequential than divisions between older and younger teachers is the divide among teachers between social liberals and social conservatives, which we capture by comparing the views of teachers who identified themselves as "born again" to those of other teachers (see appendix table A-1). As mentioned above, no less than 35 percent of the teachers identify themselves as such, and on seven issues they express views that differed significantly from those of the teaching majority. As expected, a number of the differences in opinion involve cultural issues—single-sex schooling, school prayer, mainstreaming, and assigning students to schools on the basis of family income. But a few pertain to issues on which teacher unions have taken strong positions. Socially conservative teachers are more supportive of school vouchers and tax credits and more opposed to teacher pay increases. They are also more likely to think that unions have done more harm than good in their local community. Although the divisions are intriguing, their potential to mobilize an alternative political force within the teaching profession should not be exaggerated. On many key issues—merit pay, tenure policy, teacher certification, charter schools, school accountability, pension benefits, and school spending, social conservatives do not disagree with other teachers. Any school reformer who wishes to build a movement on the back of the socially conservative members of the teaching profession will face tough sledding.

Partisan Divide

Party leaders take positions on school reform issues, and on some issues, the differences between elected officials are well known. For decades, Democratic candidates regularly support increasing funds for schools and pay for teachers, positions that Republicans support more reluctantly. Republican candidates are more likely than Democratic candidates to be aggressive proponents of school vouchers; Democratic candidates express their views more quietly. When it comes to teacher unions and collective bargaining, Democrats have few qualms while Republicans have many. Yet, on other school reform issues, the positions taken by party leaders are less polarized. Republican president George W. Bush proposed strong accountability measures as part of No Child Left Behind, but he could not have secured passage of the law without solid support from Democratic senator Edward Kennedy. Both Democrats and Republicans have backed charter schools.

The general public is also divided along partisan lines on some educational matters but not on others. On questions that fall squarely within the scope of conventional liberal and conservative thinking—more spending, higher taxes, support for unions, affirmative action—the partisan divide on education looms large, probably because those items are constantly being disputed by partisan elites. But on more specific education reform issues—merit pay, school choice, and school accountability, for example—the partisan divide within the general public is somewhere between modest and nonexistent. That may be due to the fact that most Americans have only a general idea of how the parties position themselves on any of those questions. The debates over the particulars of school reform—apart from taxes, spending, and union influence—rarely surface during the course of election campaigns. Without guidance on how the parties stand on these lesser issues, Americans are unsure about how to align their opinions with their partisan affiliation.

Admittedly, the parties sometimes take positions on these issues, although they may not devote a lot of resources to publicizing their differences with the opposition. The Democratic Party has tended to be more opposed to school vouchers and less enthusiastic about student testing, while Republicans have pushed merit pay and elimination of tenure. If teachers are attentive to more subtle party differences, they may themselves divide sharply along party lines, even more so than those outside the iron triangle. Those with a large stake in particular policy issues are more likely to notice the positions taken by political candidates and party organizations because those matters relate directly to their personal welfare. They are better positioned to pick up even weak signals about where the parties stand. While that is possible, whether it actually happens on many issues is a matter to be examined.

On the issues that provoke the most intense partisan debate—namely, taxing, spending, and union power—teachers were neither more nor less divided than the general public by their political affiliation. Democrats among the general public disproportionately support increased expenditures for education, higher taxes to fund schools, and boosts in teacher salaries (see table A-1). Among teachers, the size of the differences between Democrats and Republicans on taxing, spending, and union power are much the same: 27, 26, and 20 percentage points, respectively (see table A-2). Similarly, Republican teachers are 38 percentage points more likely than Democratic teachers to say that unions are harmful, essentially the same as the difference between Republicans and Democrats in the general population.[12]

What about issues on which the stands of the parties are less clear or less frequently publicized? Are teachers more likely to invoke their own political affiliation because they are more attuned to the positions of elected officials and party leaders on those issues? Or are they less likely to do so because their own stake in the system trumps broader political orientations? The answer depends on the policy in question. When it came to school choice, teachers are more partisan than the public. Democrats and Republicans among the general public have similar, broadly supportive views on vouchers, charter schools, tax credits for private school scholarship donations, and the expansion of online education. By contrast, Democrat and Republican teachers split sharply. The differences are especially large when it came to charter schools, tax credits, and using vouchers to expand choice. Democratic teachers are 18 percentage points less likely than Republican teachers to support vouchers and 12 percentage points less likely to support charter schools. In other words, teachers do a better job than the public at large in matching their preferences regarding school choice to their political orientation.

On those policies most directly connected to job security and working conditions, Republican and Democratic teachers see eye to eye. When their work situation is under consideration, party mattered little. Whatever their party affiliation, teachers think pretty much alike when it came to teacher tenure policy or whether school discipline should be left to the school principal, issues that divided the rest of the population along party lines. Even when Republican and Democratic teachers disagree, the differences are rarely large enough to lead either side to identify more closely with their own party than with their fellow workers.

Of special interest are Republican teachers, the cross-pressured group. On one hand, they have partisan leanings that might induce them to support policies not backed by other teachers. On the other hand, as teachers

Table 7-2. *Opinions of Democrats and Republicans among General Public and Teachers, 2011*[a]

Issue/opinion	General public		Teachers	
	Democrats	Republicans	Democrats	Republicans
Teacher policy				
Use merit pay	67	67	11	17
Use merit tenure	76	80	24	34
Allow flexible hiring	50	61*	26	31
Eliminate tenure	61	81*	31	39
Teacher unions are harmful	38	79*	15	53*
School choice				
Expand choice with universal vouchers	67	71	31	50
Use government funds for means-tested vouchers	52	47	27	31
Allow charter schools	71	75	47	58
Allow tax credit–funded scholarships	70	69	50	60
Allow online courses	64	63	49	60
Taxes and spending				
Increase spending	81	45*	86	59*
Raise taxes	47	24*	62	36*
Raise teacher pay	65	42*	91	71*
Increase teachers' share of benefit costs	63	70	24	32

a. Teachers are excluded from the general public.

* Difference in levels of support between Democrats and Republicans is statistically significant at the 0.05 level.

they have an occupational stake in policies not backed by other Republicans. Which identity has the greater hold on a group that is being pulled from both sides? As can be seen in table 7-2, there is no single answer to that question. On issues involving teacher tenure and teacher licensing, Republican teachers are teachers first, Republicans second. But on school choice and financial issues, they seem truly cross-pressured, not being clearly aligned with either side. They may not agree with fellow teachers in the opposing party, but they hardly disagree to the same extent as their fellow partisans outside the teaching profession. And yet on no choice proposal does a majority of Republican teachers stand on the opposite side of a majority of Republicans in the general public.

The pattern was different for merit pay and tenure questions. The opinions of Republican teachers again fall between those of Democratic teachers and Republicans within the general public, but Republican teachers side much more closely with their work colleagues. When it came to policies in which teachers' jobs are at stake, there is a wide gulf between Republican teachers and Republican members of the general public.

Conclusion

Teacher opinion is not monolithic. But teachers exhibit a greater level of agreement among themselves than exists within the public as a whole on issues most directly connected to teacher job security—performance pay, tenure, and compensation. General political partisanship, which has the potential to mold public attitudes on those issues, plays a somewhat lesser role within the teaching force. Admittedly, partisanship does divide teachers to a limited extent, but it remains secondary to the vested interest that the teaching force has in existing teacher policies. Party and cultural differences among teachers always pose a potential threat to the stability of the education triangle, but there is little evidence that reform pressures are building up within the teaching profession along underlying social or partisan cleavages. Nor is there much evidence that the teaching force is changing from within; younger teachers are at least as militant as older ones. There seems little danger that festering divisions among teachers will undermine the NEA-AFT alliance. If the future of the education iron triangle is in doubt, it is not because of divisions from within.

CHAPTER EIGHT

Future of the Education Iron Triangle

VARIOUS OBJECTIONS CAN be raised to the arguments advanced in this volume. In this concluding chapter we consider four of the most significant:

—The questions dictated the results.

—Teacher opinion means little because teachers lack the power to block policies that the public truly desires.

—Surveys do not capture political reality.

—Reforms will be ineffective without teacher support.

After responding to each objection we turn our attention to the future of the education iron triangle.

The Questions Dictated the Results

Many of the questions posed in your surveys focus on such matters as teacher compensation, tenure, and recruitment; school choice; and school accountability. While the views of teachers and the public may well diverge in those areas, there are many other important education policy issues—single-sex schooling, mainstreaming, affirmative action, and school prayer—where other cleavages are greater than those between teachers and the rest of the public.

It is true that we give special attention to certain issues that divide teacher opinion from that of the general public. But those issues deserve special attention, because they dominate school politics today. Teacher prerogatives and school choice provoked bitter controversy in New Jersey in 2009, and the same topics dominated campaigns in elections across the country in 2010. An uproar broke out in the state capitol buildings when proposals to limit the reach of collective bargaining were introduced in Wisconsin and Indiana. In 2013, a strike over merit pay and charter schools took place in Chicago, and the same issues provoked intense debate in New York City's mayoral campaign. The battle over Common Core State Standards is only the latest round in the long-running school accountability fight. The issues central to this volume are central to the country's education agenda.

Teachers Lack Political Power

This exploration of teacher opinion assumes that a small segment of the public—no more than 2 to 3 percent—has the power to block policies that the public truly desires. Teachers do not have the money and power of bankers and oil barons, or the prestige of the medical profession, or the sheer numbers represented by the Association for the Advancement of Retired Persons. To equate them to some of the most potent interests in American politics is woefully misleading.

Admittedly, teachers are too few to exercise power by strength of numbers alone, and no one teacher has the resources of the captains of industry. But the National Education Association and the American Federation of Teachers have successfully recruited a large majority of teachers into their ranks and have many tools at hand to facilitate political action. In thirty-four states, school districts must bargain with teacher union representatives, and in only eight states are they prohibited from doing so. Collective bargaining gives teachers privileged access to decisionmakers outside the normal political processes. As recently as 1960, collective bargaining was forbidden in almost all political jurisdictions on the grounds that it led to the making of law by an unconstitutional procedure.[1] Since legal restrictions on collective bargaining were lifted throughout most of the country, teacher unions have become a formidable political force.

For example, in twenty states, school districts collect dues levied by teacher unions directly from a teacher's paycheck unless the teacher specifically requests otherwise. Only eight states forbid the practice. In California, dues constitute 2 percent of teacher salaries. Those dues provide the unions with the deep pockets needed to fund lobbyists in state capitols, information campaigns promoting union-favored policies, and charitable contributions to other, like-minded groups. Unless a teacher objects, money collected from paychecks can also be used for overt political activities, and teacher unions are among the groups that contribute the most to candidates running for national, state, and school district elections.[2] In a 2002 study of group power in state politics, teacher associations ranked second only to chambers of commerce.[3] To the extent that unions represent teacher opinion—and all the evidence that we have explored suggests that they do—teachers wield considerable political power.

Surveys Do Not Capture Political Reality

Public opinion is ill-defined, amorphous, and incoherent. Individuals do not hold consistent opinions on related topics. Majorities simultaneously want higher spending, lower taxes, and reductions in the size of government deficits. They provide different answers to the same question when it is posed at different times. Further, voters may say that they favor a policy in a survey but then vote against a similar proposal in a state referendum. Take the case of school vouchers, for example. In California, Washington, Michigan, and Colorado, the public expressed strong support for school vouchers, yet the voters in each case turned down the opportunity to set up state voucher programs.

This argument has considerable force. When the opinions of individual citizens are ascertained, they often are vague, poorly formulated, and inconsistent.[4] Our own data reveal a fair amount of volatility in the views expressed by individual respondents, some of whom participated in multiple years. Of those asked to grade the nation's public schools in both 2008 and 2009, for example, only 59 percent assign the same grade both years. Of those who gave a grade of "A" or "B" in 2008, 46 percent award a grade of "C" or lower in 2009.

Individual respondents also express different views on controversial policy issues across survey years. Among those who either completely or somewhat supported merit pay in 2008, 34 percent do not support it one year later. Conversely, 29 percent of respondents who either completely or somewhat opposed the policy in 2008 do not express the same opposition the next year. Similar churning is evident in the responses to questions concerning single-sex public schools, charter schools, and national standards.

However, the flip-flop that characterizes as much as one-third of individual responses does not produce equally large fluctuations in aggregate public opinion. On the contrary, the percentage of Americans holding to a particular point of view typically remains stable from one year to the next. On two-thirds of the domestic issues studied by political scientists Benjamin Page and Robert Shapiro, opinion does not change by more than 5 percentage points, despite the fact that many years may separate the fielding of different surveys. In the aftermath of major events—wars, economic recessions, or terrorist attacks—the views of the public as a whole may change abruptly and dramatically. More commonly, though, public opinion either holds firm or eases slowly in one direction or another.[5]

Aggregate public opinion on education issues also is fairly stable over time. Between 2007 and 2012, we posed the same or similar twenty-three questions on two or more occasions (see table 8-1).[6] For ten of the twenty-three questions, the difference in aggregate responses between the first and last occasions on which the question was posed is no more than 6 percentage points. For nineteen of the twenty-three questions, the responses were within 10 percentage points of one another. The topics includes such key issues as accountability, merit pay for teachers, the effects of teacher unions on school quality, the desirability of teacher certification, raising taxes to finance more education spending, single-sex schooling, and mainstreaming students with behavioral and emotional problems. In only the following four instances do we identify a substantively important change in public opinion during that period:

—Support for using student test scores in teacher tenure decisions increases by 10 percentage points. However, no corresponding increase in public enthusiasm for using test scores to determine teacher salaries is observed.

—Support for using tax credits to fund private school scholarships for low-income students rises by 14 percentage points. However, increase in support for other school choice options, such as school vouchers and charter schools, does not change significantly.

—Support for raising teacher salaries declines by 18 percentage points among those informed of current salary levels in their state. However, there is no corresponding drop in support for higher salaries among those who were not told current salary levels.

—Support for affirmative action for students from low-income families in school assignments increases by 16 percentage points. However, this

Table 8-1. *Public Opinion on Selected School Issues, 2007–12*[a]

Issue/opinion	2007	2008	2009	2010	2011	2012
Teacher policy						
Use merit pay	64	61	61	65	64	–
Use merit tenure	–	–	72	–	74	82
Allow flexible hiring	59	–	–	–	57	61
Eliminate tenure	–	–	64	65	70	63
Teacher unions are harmful	–	–	53	54	56	58
School choice						
Expand choice with universal vouchers	–	–	–	–	64	60
Use government funds for means-tested vouchers	57	50	45	42	50	49
Allow charter schools	76	72	70	70	70	73
Allow tax credit–funded scholarships	–	–	63	69	70	77
Allow online courses	–	–	59	69	65	–
Accountability						
Require annual testing	–	–	–	84	88	84
Use common standards/test	–	69	72	–	72	–
Use test for grade promotion	90	–	–	87	86	85
Require graduation test	89	–	–	90	86	86
Taxes and spending						
Increase spending	–	61	46	63	65	63
Increase spending (with information)	–	51	38	–	45	43
Raise taxes	–	–	–	29	35	35
Raise teacher pay	–	69	56	59	55	64
Raise teacher pay (with information)	–	54	40	42	40	36
Increase teachers' share of benefit costs	–	–	–	–	64	69
Cultural issues						
Allow single-sex schools	–	60	54	–	59	–
Grant principal final disciplinary authority	–	41	–	–	–	–
Allow silent prayer	–	68	–	–	–	–
Diversity						
Use family income to assign students	–	21	–	–	37	–
Separate classes for disturbed students	–	72	–	–	65	–

a. Each year includes all responses adjusted with post-stratification weights for representation. A dash indicates that the question was not asked that year.

question is asked at only two points in time, the second time with an alternative wording that respondents may have viewed more favorably (see chapter 2), calling into question whether the change was genuine.

In addition, support for school vouchers for low-income students declined by 15 percentage points between 2007 and 2010, only to recover 7 percentage points by 2012. The downturn may have been driven by the strong Democratic campaign against vouchers during the 2008 presidential election, and the recovery may have been driven by the Republican revival in the 2010 off-year election. But no similar trend line is evident for other school choice options.

Overall, public opinion on education issues barely budges between 2007 and 2012 rather than shifting sharply either for or against school reform. As energetic as proponents have been in pushing school reform and teacher unions have been in defending the prerogatives of their members, the weight of public opinion remains largely the same.

Why is aggregate opinion so stable when individuals appear to change their minds regularly? Undoubtedly, part of the explanation is measurement error. Some of those answering our survey questions may have misread or misunderstood the questions in one year or the other, so their opinion seemed to have changed when in fact it did not. That kind of error balances itself out, as mistakes by one individual offset opposite errors by another. When that is the case, aggregate opinion remains stable even when individual responses fluctuate.

But it seems unlikely that one-third of our respondents would make such mistakes, and a substantial body of research on political behavior suggests that something else is going on as well. One prominent theory emphasizes the influence of public discourse. When people answer a survey item, they often draw on recent media reports or conversations with friends, relatives, or co-workers. Individual responses, then, may vary from week to week as people are exposed to different claims. Collective opinion, however, remains constant as long as the general discourse does. If that theory is correct, then opinion in the aggregate changes only when public discourse shifts—because of a major event, new information, or a political change, such as endorsement (or condemnation) of a policy by a popular political figure.[7]

That, of course, is what happens when an issue is put up for popular vote in a referendum. Those trying to influence the outcome present facts, arguments, and the views of presumably popular political leaders. A favorite tactic in debates over vouchers has been to claim that the law would allow the funding of Islamic schools attended by potential terrorists or Christian schools organized by bizarre figures such as David Koresh, who immolated himself and his followers in Waco, Texas, during a raid by the FBI. Opposition to vouchers by Democratic political elites also undermines voter support. Referendums are often won by the side that does the best job of mobilizing its supporters, and those opposed to an innovation are often better organized, more focused, and more persuasive at identifying harms to identifiable groups than those who can offer only the prospect of a better future for a group as ill-defined as "future generations of students."

But even if a survey cannot predict the outcome of a referendum, it can provide clues to the general predisposition of the population. It may take some event—or some organized group able to provide a counterweight to teacher organizations—to galvanize public opinion into action.

Reforms Will Be Ineffective without Teacher Support

Education takes place within classrooms, and the most important figure in that classroom is the teacher. The importance of any differences between teacher and public opinion pales in comparison with the importance of that reality. If school reform is to take place, it must win the backing of those who are responsible for its execution. Change must take place with the consent and cooperation of teachers if it is to occur at all.

In important ways we agree with—indeed, we affirm the force of—this argument. A reform agenda opposed by a sizable majority of the teacher workforce, even if it is enacted, will prove difficult to implement. According to what has been called "capture theory," attempts at industry regulation generally falter because the regulated eventually "capture" the regulator.[8] Agencies charged with responsibility to protect the public interest eventually succumb to the steady, drip-by-drip resistance of those inside the iron triangle who are supposed to be under the agency's control. The agency may fight the triangle when it is first established in response to an industry scandal. But while public attention wanes and elected representatives turn to other issues, the iron triangle never ceases to use its friends and allies to revise, redesign, and water down regulations that it regards as draconian. No rule can be written that is not open to reinterpretation in the course of its implementation, at which point those inside the iron triangle have the political advantage. They have firsthand knowledge of the specific harms that the industry is suffering and can argue convincingly for revision, reconsideration, and exceptions. If capture theory is correct, then regulation often has less impact than anticipated by those who write the rule.

When the general public is aroused by a major crisis, policymakers can seek to correct matters in one of two ways: imposing new regulations or introducing new forms of competition. The regulatory strategy is generally perceived to present the quicker, easier solution, as it attempts only to reform the iron triangle, not break it apart. But capture theory suggests that the regulatory strategy often promises more than it delivers.[9] The classic instance is the Interstate Commerce Commission (ICC), originally established in 1887 to check the power of railroad barons who allegedly were exploiting farmers in the West. With the passage of time, the ICC fell under the influence of the railroad industry itself, which used its muscle to block its rising rival, the trucking industry. The ICC's powers were eventually curbed in the 1970s, when its decisions grew increasingly bizarre and a deregulation movement swept through Washington, and in 1995 the country's first independent regulatory commission was swept into the dustbin. Since its demise, the railroad industry, which had grown moribund under ICC regulation, has found new life in an era when concern about global warming has put the brakes on trucking interests.[10]

Like the ICC, many regulatory agencies in existence today were established at a time when the public demanded that something be done about abuses of privilege by corporations, agencies, or unions within a particular industry. Amid the massive bank failures of the Great Depression, the Federal Deposit Insurance Corporation was set up to protect savings accounts from future disasters. Yet its operations, by curtailing competition, have often served the interests of the banking industry more than the consuming public. The Federal Energy Regulatory Commission was established to protect the consumer from manipulation of energy prices, but much of the time its activities serve to protect the prerogatives of existing industry powers. The Securities and Exchange Commission, created during the New Deal as a mechanism for halting Wall Street abuses, in recent times became more the servant of Wall Street, unable to check even some of its most egregious actions. The agency supervised Enron investment strategies so loosely that it was unable to limit actions that eventually bankrupted the firm.[11] Nor did it perform the standard due diligence needed to detect the $50 billion pyramid scheme marketed by Wall Street insider Bernard Madoff. Its failure to keep a careful watch on credit markets contributed to the financial crisis of 2008.

Agencies seeking to regulate the education iron triangle face similar obstacles. Because education professionals control what happens on the ground, they have innumerable ways of resisting regulation. When the Seattle school board proposed to use student performance as a basis for teacher evaluations, teachers refused to administer the tests. Although the board threatened retaliation, the teachers went unpunished and the board later softened its policies.[12] On occasion, local resistance can lead to major scandals, such as the massive 2012 cheating scandal in the Atlanta public schools that culminated in the indictment of the district superintendent.

District tolerance of teacher walkouts is not unique to Seattle, and cheating on standardized tests is probably not limited to the city of Atlanta.[13] However, the primary obstacle to effective education regulation is not illegal behavior. Much more significant are perfectly legal efforts to water down regulations or obtain exceptions to the rule. The most telling example is the No Child Left Behind Act (NCLB), which, for the first time, placed a federal regulatory framework around the core operations of local school districts in 2002, only to see those regulations blocked, watered down, and rendered ineffective. When NCLB required that all students reach proficiency by the year 2014, state education departments set standards at levels much lower than those set by national and international organizations.[14] When NCLB required that parents of students attending a failing school be given the opportunity to move their child to a new school, many local districts designed procedures that made it difficult for parents to exercise that choice.[15] When NCLB required the reconstitution of schools that failed for five consecutive years, most districts ignored recommended options such as dismissing relevant school staff or converting a failing school into a charter school; instead, they exploited a loophole that allowed them to pursue less aggressive options, such as adopting a new curriculum or hiring a state-trained "coach" to advise the school's staff.[16] More generally, efforts to introduce merit pay plans and tighten teacher tenure rules have encountered strong and successful resistance not only in Chicago but throughout the country.[17]

By 2013 the U.S. Department of Education had waived most of the NCLB requirements for thirty-seven states and the District of Columbia, provided that they accept a new regulatory framework that requires them, among other things, to develop teacher and principal evaluation systems based substantially on student test scores and use the results of evaluations in making personnel decisions. Whether this new framework will prove more effective than NCLB's remains to be seen, but there already are signs of trouble. In June 2013, the evaluation system requirements had generated enough resistance that the secretary of education announced that states could request permission to delay their implementation until the 2016–17 school year, a proposal first advanced by Randi Weingarten, the president of the American Federation of Teachers (AFT).[18]

If regulation were the only mechanism by which the public can exercise control over its education system, then critics might well be right to say that reforms must be acceptable to teachers in order to succeed. But regulation is not the only strategy available. The alternative—breaking monopoly control through the introduction of competition—is the strategy that has proven to be the most successful in other industries, having repeatedly transformed them despite aggressive efforts on the part of existing producers to preserve their monopoly power. Unlike regulation, the introduction of competition does not require the consent of the regulated. It can be imposed from above and eventually work its will, despite objections by those within the iron triangle.

Two examples illustrate the capacity of competition to break iron triangles. The first involves the airlines. In 1934, a scandal involving the misuse of postal funds coupled with concerns about airline safety led to the establishment of the Civil Aeronautics Authority, later subdivided into the Civil Aeronautics Administration and the Civil Aeronautics Board (CAB), which was given control over entry, exit, and pricing within the industry. As public attention wandered to other matters, the dominant airlines, together with their employee unions, captured the board and used its authority to restrict entry of new competitors on the grounds that they would compromise public safety. But as air travel costs escalated and researchers called attention to the consumer costs of regulation, Congress called CAB's role into question and in 1984 phased the agency out of existence. It became much easier for new companies to enter the industry, traditional alliances were completely disrupted, airline prices tumbled, and air travel became a way of life for average Americans.[19] The airline iron triangle, as it had existed, was broken, never to be reconstructed on its original terms.

Competition also transformed the communications industry. Until 1984 the American Telephone and Telegraph Company (AT&T), subject to the authority of the Federal Communications Commission, controlled all interstate and, through its "Baby Bell" system of regional subsidiaries, intrastate telecommunications as well. When a 1984 federal court decision broke up the AT&T–Baby Bell alliance, competition broke out among the Bells. Some became so powerful that they threatened to create new oligopolies, but Congress stepped in and President Bill Clinton signed into law the Telecommunications Act of 1996, which opened the industry to new competitors. The dizzying world of technological innovation—with its cell phones, smartphones, Internet connections, and instant, low-cost international communications—transformed the industry far beyond the expectations of any of those involved in the deregulatory process.[20]

Neither AT&T nor the railroads and major airlines welcomed the competition that came with deregulation. When airline deregulation came, the industry was forced to adjust whether executives and employees liked the idea or not, as the alternative was bankruptcy forced by competition from enterprising newcomers. Similarly, telecommunications were restructured not because AT&T stockholders and employees were induced to participate but because new approaches were introduced into the marketplace

The education iron triangle is little different. When competition threatens monopoly control, school districts and teacher unions fight back just as aggressively as the railroads, the airlines, and AT&T did. But if they fail to block the entrance of new competitors, they must adjust or lose out to the competition. Once oligopolistic power disappears from the marketplace, the oligopolists' political power is severely weakened as well. If large-scale competition is introduced, the government will not need to persuade teachers to go along with reforms, as teachers will be struggling to keep their jobs if students move elsewhere.

One question remains, however. Is there any force on the political scene strong enough to introduce so much competition into the system of K-12 education that it would break the monopoly power of teachers, teacher unions, and school districts? Or is this triangle made not of iron, but of steel?

The Triangle's Future

Unlike the proverbial diamond, iron triangles are not necessarily forever. Under enough force they can be mangled, bent out of shape, or split apart. When they begin to rust, they are all the more vulnerable. By exposing the iron triangle to the open air, information can corrode a political iron triangle. As was shown in chapter 4, public enthusiasm for positions espoused by teachers and their representatives declines both when the public acquires information on the actual cost of education in a school district and when it learns current salary levels teachers receive in the state. Public support for teacher-backed policies also declines when the public is told how well its district's student performances compare with those of other districts statewide and nationally. If Common Core State Standards and other efforts to convey the actual performance level of students in each school district should prove successful, insider resistance to school reform might be overcome by broader political forces.

Attacks on the education iron triangle are occurring with increasing frequency. In Florida, Governor Jeb Bush pushed a broad range of educational innovations—a highly visible school accountability system, school vouchers for both low-income students and those in need of special education, performance pay for teachers, and a statewide virtual school. In New York City, Mayor Michael Bloomberg and Chancellor Joel Klein tried out a plethora of innovations—elimination of seniority as the basis for teacher assignments, performance pay, small high schools of choice, charter schools, digital learning, and much more. In Indiana in 2011, Governor Mitch Daniels instituted new teacher and school accountability systems, an expansive private school choice program, and limitations on teacher collective bargaining rights, among other reforms.

More important than any of those developments, however, are three great controversies—and one innovation in standards and accountability—that have pitted prominent political figures against organized labor.

In 2007 in Washington, D.C., a new mayor, Adrian Fenty, asked Michelle Rhee to revamp the district's schools, which had long been among the lowest performing in the nation. Rhee insisted on a performance pay program for teachers, welcomed the city's growing school choice movement—including both vouchers and charters—and actually removed some teachers for poor performance. The local teacher union, severely weakened by a corruption scandal, called in help from AFT's national offices. Eventually, the local union rallied its constituents and helped to defeat Mayor Fenty, driving Superintendent Rhee from office. For months, even years, the story of the bitter battle between a hard-nosed superintendent and an entrenched union made headlines nationwide.

Still, that was small news compared with the uproar that occurred in Wisconsin in 2011 when Governor Scott Walker, with the help of the Republican majority in the state legislature, cut teacher pension and health care benefits, banned the automatic withdrawal of union dues from employee paychecks (unless the teacher specifically requested otherwise), and narrowed the range of topics that were subject to union bargaining. All Democratic members of the state senate refused to attend legislative sessions, an illegal action that prevented the formation of a quorum. To prevent police from dragooning them into attending, they left the state altogether. Only after some legislative sleight-of-hand did the governor succeed in securing the law's passage. The teacher union responded by collecting enough signatures to force a recall election. The effort to oust Walker won the backing of Democrats across the country, including explicit support from President Obama. Many thought Walker's political future was short, but in the summer of 2012 he squeaked through.

The most telling event, however, was the Chicago strike described in chapter 1. In this instance, a big-city teacher union picked a fight not with a Republican or a political independent but with Rahm Emmanuel, a Democratic political insider with close ties to the president of the United States.

Such controversies begin to wear. The public becomes increasingly well-informed and aware that something is amiss, and information, as we have seen, only widens the teacher-public divide. Furthermore, the Chicago conflict involved leaders of the political party with which teacher unions have been closely allied. When an iron triangle takes on major political figures in both parties, it plays high-stakes politics.

It is too soon to say whether the introduction of Common Core State Standards will change school reform politics. But if the findings in chapter 6 translate into real-world politics, teacher unions must worry about growing public uneasiness if all districts are compared with one another on a rigorous, common standard that allows the members of the public to see how well their own district ranks nationally. Not only will satisfaction with local schools decline but support for universal school vouchers and charter schools can be expected to increase, introducing the competition that poses a potential threat to the current school district monopoly.

If that development gathers force, there could be serious consequences for teacher unions if the triangle feels the heat of the not-so-dying embers of the racial conflagration that once engulfed American schools. Should the teacher-public divide become an even more intense division between teachers and racial or ethnic minority groups, teacher power could lose its triangular shape.

Opinion among Teachers and Racial/Ethnic Minorities

Currently, attitudes among teachers (who are predominantly white) and among major racial and ethnic minority groups overlap on many important issues. They agree that schools need more money, that teachers should have higher salaries, that schools should be held accountable, and that teacher unions are more beneficial than harmful. But consider the following opinions and assessments (see table 8-2):

—The average African American is less than half as likely as the average teacher to give the nation's schools an "A" or "B" grade.

—School vouchers (whether offered universally or to low-income families) are supported by at least 67 percent of African Americans and Hispanics but by fewer than 40 percent of teachers.

—The formation of charter schools is favored by 76 percent of African Americans and 69 percent of Hispanics but by just 54 percent of the teaching force.

—Tax credits to fund private school scholarships for low-income students are favored by 80 percent of African Americans and 81 percent of Hispanics but by only 51 percent of teachers.[21]

—Sixty-four percent of African Americans and 75 percent of Hispanics support merit pay, but only 16 percent of teachers do. Similarly large

Table 8-2. *Policy Opinions and Evaluations of Teachers,*
African Americans, and Hispanics, 2011[a]

Percent

Issue/opinion	Teacher	Black	Hispanic
Evaluation of national schools			
Give grade A or B	38	16	37
Give grade C	47	59	46
Give grade D or F	15	25	17
Teacher policy			
Use merit pay	16	64	75
Use merit tenure	29	78	83
Allow flexible hiring	30	60	58
Eliminate tenure	35	44	56
Teacher unions are harmful	32	23	38
School choice			
Expand choice with universal vouchers	38	67	81
Use government funds for means-tested vouchers	27	68	68
Allow charter schools	54	76	69
Allow tax credit–funded scholarships	51	80	81
Allow online courses	56	73	76
Accountability			
Require testing	65	91	92
Use common standards/test	60	69	67
Use test for grade promotion	72	82	93
Require graduation test	77	79	89
Taxes and spending			
Increase spending	71	78	78
Increase spending (with information)	53	62	55
Raise taxes	49	42	44
Raise teacher pay	80	79	65
Raise teacher pay (with information)	80	62	53
Increase teachers' share of benefit costs	29	54	68
Cultural issues			
Allow single-sex schools	71	68	60
Grant principal final disciplinary authority	57	42	43
Allow time for silent prayer	58	86	65
Diversity			
Use family income to assign students	37	58	58
Separate classes for disturbed students	67	62	48

a. Calculated from oversamples of these subgroups in the 2011 survey using poststratification weights.

differences between minorities and teachers are evident on the questions of whether teachers should be required to demonstrate success in raising student achievement before receiving tenure and whether schools should be granted greater flexibility to hire teachers who lack traditional education credentials.

—Fifty-four percent of African Americans and 68 percent of Hispanics think that teachers should pay 20 percent of the cost of their retirement and health care benefits, but just 29 percent of teachers are willing to accept that sacrifice.

These are all large differences, and they run the full gamut of contemporary policy questions, from school choice, merit pay, and tenure policy to school accountability.

Both teachers and members of minority groups identify disproportionately with the Democratic Party, which is committed to a higher level of education spending than is favored by most Republicans. The alliance between teachers and minorities within the Democratic coalition can be held together as long as education problems are defined as the by-product of inadequate funding. While successful in the past, today that strategy is becoming problematic due to the ever-rising costs of public education, the explosion in other types of public expenditures (on health care services, pension outlays, incarceration, and so forth), and the unprecedented levels of debt held in peacetime by not only the federal government but also the states and local municipalities. At a time when the public is resistant to broad-based tax increases, the money needed to stitch together a fraying coalition has become increasingly hard to find.

In a key respect, teacher unions owe their collective bargaining rights to the civil rights movement. Before 1960, strikes by public school teachers were illegal, and even today such actions violate the law in many jurisdictions. Collective bargaining within the public sector was widely seen as inappropriate—and possibly even unconstitutional—because government policy would no longer be set independently by officials elected by the public but through a process in which a private entity, the teacher union, had special access. Not until Martin Luther King enshrined nonviolent disobedience as a civil rights strategy did the teacher strike become acceptable. The ties between the civil rights movement and the early push to organize teachers were personified by union leader Al Shanker, who had participated in nonviolent protest actions, including illegal sit-ins and other demonstrations.

Although Shanker and his union later used the strike to break an attempt by minority groups to gain control of neighborhood schools in New York City, that was merely a temporary disruption of what has since become a stable alliance. Teacher unions support school integration, affirmative action, and a strong emphasis on educational equity in exchange for support from civil rights organizations for key items on the union agenda—teacher tenure, the single salary schedule, and tight limits on school choice. As a concrete indicator of the alliance, teacher unions contribute substantial sums to minority and civil rights interest groups. In its fiscal year ending in 2012, the AFT donated nearly a half-million dollars from its membership dues to twenty-five different civil rights or minority group organizations.[22] Since many of the civil rights groups are small and have limited access to other fund streams, that fiscal support provides valuable glue that keeps the alliance intact.

A solid civil rights–union phalanx has major benefits for teacher unions. At the grassroots level, African Americans and Hispanics support vouchers, tax credits, charters, merit pay, tenure reform, and accountability. Yet traditional civil rights organizations have regularly backed teacher union positions on those issues. For example, the NAACP has vigorously and repeatedly opposed the federally funded school voucher program in Washington, D.C.; it joined the teacher union in a lawsuit against charter school operations in New York City; and its Jacksonville, Florida, chapter opposed a performance pay plan for teachers, saying that it would lead to the removal of troublesome children from classrooms.

Still, traditional civil rights groups are increasingly being challenged by new organizations—such as the Black Alliance for Educational Options and parent trigger and numerous other local parents' groups—that back charter schools and voucher programs that disproportionately serve the minority community. For unions, such groups remain small clouds on a distant horizon. If their constituents should become activated, however, the ingredients for a major storm are already evident within the interstices of public opinion. It is, of course, one thing to have the public predisposed in a certain direction and quite another to organize and mobilize that public. Iron triangles bet that they can wait out temporary shifts in the political mood because the leadership necessary to organize broad swaths of the public around a commonly held set of policy views usually dissipates. Quite likely, it will take a more fundamental change in the climate in which education policy is debated to oxidize the education iron triangle.

APPENDIX A
Data Collection and Analysis

THE FINDINGS REPORTED in this volume are based on seven annual surveys of nationally representative samples of the U.S. adult population conducted from 2007 to 2013. The surveys were conducted under the auspices of Harvard University's Program on Education Policy and Governance (PEPG) and *Education Next: A Journal of Opinion and Research*. The surveys were administered by the polling firm Knowledge Networks (KN). KN maintains a nationally representative panel of adult survey respondents, obtained though list-assisted, random-digit-dialing sampling techniques, who agree to participate in a limited number of online surveys. Although surveys are administered online, the sample is not limited to current computer owners or users with Internet access because KN offers panel members without access free Internet access and a WebTV device that connects to a telephone and television. When recruiting for the panel, KN sends out an advance mailing and follows up with at least fifteen dialing attempts. The panel is updated quarterly. Detailed information about the maintenance of the KN panel, the protocols used to administer surveys, and the comparability of online and telephone surveys is available at www.knowledgenetworks.com/quality/. Participants in the *Education Next*–PEPG surveys are randomly sampled from KN's panel of respondents. Several of the surveys included oversamples of various subgroups (for example, parents and teachers). For each survey, post-stratification population weights are calculated in order to adjust for survey nonresponse as well as for subgroup oversampling. Those weights ensure that the observed demographic characteristics of the final sample match the known characteristics of the national adult population. All analyses presented in the text are based on weighted data. Reported percentages do not always add to 100 as a result of rounding to the nearest percentage point.

Because respondents' geographic locations were known prior to the time that the survey was administered, it was possible to link respondents to personalized information about local schools either for use in the survey or for analysis after data were collected. So, for example, we obtained information on the amount of per-pupil spending in respondents' local school districts. In some cases that information was used to compare perceptions of spending to actual spending; in other cases, the information was provided to respondents as they completed the questionnaire. In order to secure accurate matches between respondents and information about local districts, we matched survey respondents to school districts using either census blocks or zip codes. When we relied on zip codes, we could not match some respondents to a unique school district. For such respondents we calculated the average per-pupil spending levels for each district that served the relevant zip code, weighted by the districts' population size. For the experiments involving teacher salaries, only state-level data were available. We were able to match all survey respondents to the states in which they resided. Data on per-pupil spending came from the Local Education Agency Finance Survey of the National Center for Education Statistics' Common Core of Data. Data on teacher salaries came from the American Federation of Teachers publication "Survey and Analysis of Teacher Salary Trends." In each survey, the most recent financial data available were used.

The survey administered in 2011 included many more questions, carried out more experiments, and oversampled many more groups than previous iterations of the survey, allowing for a more extended examination of many issues than in previous years. As a result, the data reported in this volume lean heavily on the 2011 results, even though it makes use of data from other years when doing so illuminates a topic. If results come from a year other than 2011, that fact is specifically indicated in the text; otherwise the reported numbers are from the 2011 survey.

—*2007.* The 2007 survey was conducted between February 16 and March 15, 2007. Data were collected from a nationally representative stratified sample of 2,000 adults (ages 18 years and older). The sample consists of 1,482 non-Hispanic whites, 233 non-Hispanic blacks, and

171 Hispanics. The survey oversampled parents of school-age children, who constitute 811 members of the total sample.

—*2008.* The 2008 survey was conducted between February 16 and March 15, 2008. The sample consists of 2,546 non-Hispanic whites, 250 non-Hispanic blacks, and 239 Hispanics. It includes an oversample of approximately 700 public school teachers.

—*2009.* The 2009 survey was conducted between February 25 and March 13, 2009. The total sample includes a nationally representative sample of 1,594 adults (ages 18 years and older) and oversamples of 709 public school teachers and 948 residents of Florida (the latter for analyses not reported here). The combined sample of 3,251 respondents consists of 2,153 non-Hispanic whites, 434 non-Hispanic blacks, and 481 Hispanics.

—*2010.* The 2010 survey was conducted between May 11 and June 8, 2010. The total sample includes a nationally representative sample of 1,184 adults (ages 18 years and older) and oversamples of 684 public school teachers and 908 residents of zip codes in which a charter school was located during the 2009–10 school year. The total sample of 2,776 adults consists of 2,038 non-Hispanic whites, 280 non-Hispanic blacks, and 263 Hispanics.

—*2011.* The 2011 survey was conducted between April 15 and May 4, 2011. The total sample of 5,251 includes oversamples of public school teachers (836), parents of school-age children (1,615), residents of zip codes in which a charter school was located during the 2009–10 school year (1,837), African Americans (1,043), Hispanics (1,027), and affluent individuals (846; see definition below). Respondents were randomly assigned to one of two versions of the questionnaire, one asking about schools in local communities, the other about schools across the nation. The 2011 results used in this volume, with the exception of chapter 4, are based on the half of the sample assigned to answer questions about schools across the nation. This sample consists of 2,619 respondents, including oversamples of public school teachers (436), parents of school-age children (818), residents of zip codes in which a charter school was located during the 2009–10 school year (928), African Americans (506), Hispanics (509), and affluent individuals (412). Altogether, this yields a sample of 2,183 nonteachers (83 percent) and 436 teachers (17 percent).

Respondents could elect to complete the survey in English or Spanish. In order to isolate the views of the affluent, we identified Americans with at least a B.A. degree or its equivalent whose household income placed them in the top 10 percent of the income distribution in their state. Of the sample of 412 respondents, 45 percent were men; 58 percent had an advanced degree beyond the B.A.; 28 percent were parents of school-age children; 84 percent were married; 85 percent were white; 2 percent were African American; 4 percent were Hispanic; and 8 percent were of another race/ethnicity or from multiple racial/ethnic backgrounds.

—*2012.* The 2012 survey was conducted between April 27 and May 11, 2012. Those interviewed consist of a nationally representative sample of 2,993 adults (ages 18 years and older) and representative oversamples of 461 public school teachers, 794 parents of school-age children, 550 African Americans, and 501 Hispanics. Respondents could elect to complete the survey in English or Spanish.

—*2013.* The 2013 survey was conducted in June 2013. The total sample of 5,569 respondents includes 2,005 respondents who were selected to represent the U.S. adult population, plus oversamples of teachers, parents, African Americans, and Hispanics. Sample sizes for groups that were oversampled (including observations that were initially selected as representative of the U.S. population) were as follows: 787 public school teachers, 1,701 parents of school-age children, 1,205 African Americans, and 1,337 Hispanics. Respondents could elect to complete the survey in English or Spanish.

Data Analysis

Two different types of analyses are reported—bivariate analyses of observational data and experimental analyses. Bivariate analysis reports simple differences in the distribution of opinion between groups—such as the differences between the public and the affluent as well as the differences between the public and teachers. Bivariate analyses also are used to report simple changes in public opinion over time. One concern with simple bivariate comparisons is that other factors not used in the comparison may account for differences across groups. To address that concern, we also examined the bivariate comparisons found in chapters 2, 3, and 5 using multivariate regression analysis, which allows us to control for the following characteristics simultaneously: age, income, education, race/ethnicity, gender, home ownership, whether the respondent has a school-age child, whether the respondent is a teacher, whether the respondent describes himself or herself as a "born again" Christian, and partisanship. Although the magnitude of the differences presented in the text shift depending on whether bivariate comparison or multivariate regression is used, the substantive results are generally the same. Our experimental analyses compare randomly selected segments of a sample with one another. The difference between the two segments of the sample can be attributed to the wording of the question, as it is assumed that each segment does not differ from the other apart from random fluctuation. When interpreting the results of both bivariate and experimental analyses, we consider a difference between two groups to be statistically significant if there is less than a 5 percent chance that we would have observed a difference of that size as a result of chance if the two segments in fact held the same views.

See appendix tables A-1 and A-2 for the social divides within the general public and the teaching profession, respectively. Column 1 in both tables indicates the percentage difference in the opinions of teachers and the general public. Appendix B provides the wording of survey questions mentioned in this monograph.

Table A-1. *Social Cleavages in Opinions on Education Issues within General Public, 2011*[a]

Issue/opinion	Teachers (1)	Parents (2)	Homeowners (3)	Affluent (4)	"Born again" (5)	Older (6)	Democrats (7)	Blacks (8)	Hispanics (9)
Teacher policy									
Use merit pay	-50*	4	0	-5	3	11*	-1	1	13*
Use merit tenure	-46*	2	-2	-5	7*	9	-5	6	11*
Allow flexible hiring	-28*	-4	-7	15*	1	-2	-11*	5	3
Eliminate tenure	-37*	5	19*	8	5*	9*	-18*	-32*	-20*
Teacher unions are harmful	-25*	8	25*	12*	5*	20*	-41*	-43*	-28*
School choice									
Expand choice with universal vouchers	-27*	17*	-16*	-10	3	-10	-5	9	22*
Use government funds for means-tested vouchers	-24*	-1	-22*	-1	12*	-13*	5	25*	26*
Allow charter schools	-17*	6	-4	6	4	-10	-5	7	1
Allow tax credit–funded scholarships	-20*	12*	-15*	-4	9*	-14*	0	15*	15*
Allow online courses	-9	9*	-11*	-14*	6*	-5*	0	11*	15*
Accountability									
Require annual testing	-24*	-2	-2	-2	4*	6*	-1	4	5
Use common standards/test	-12*	0	8*	2	-4*	9*	-7*	-5	-6
Use test for grade promotion	-15*	-5	4	1	2	14*	-8*	-3	8*
Require graduation test	-10*	-4	5	4	2	9*	-6	-7	3

Taxes and spending								
Increase spending	6	13*	-6	0	-28*	36*	18*	**18***
Raise taxes	14*	6	6	-3	-12*	23*	10*	**12***
Raise teacher pay	**26***	0	2	2	-13*	22*	29*	**16***
Increase teachers' share of benefit costs	**-37***	-5	7	3	20*	-7	-12*	1
Cultural issues								
Allow single-sex schools	12*	-7	8	10*	9*	-6	11	3
Grant principal final disciplinary authority	**16***	**-8***	NA	5	7	-11*	1	3
Allow silent prayer	**-11***	-3	NA	43*	16*	-17*	19*	-2
Diversity								
Use family income to assign students	0	-12*	-4	7*	-5*	23*	29*	30*
Separate classes for disturbed students	2	0	-1	4	14*	-9	-6	-20*

a. African Americans and Hispanics are each contrasted with whites. Democrats are contrasted with Republicans (partisan leaners excluded). "Older" refers to the oldest third (age 56 or older) contrasted with the youngest third (age 41 or younger). All other categories show the identified group contrasted with the remainder of the public. Evangelicals are those who identified themselves as "born again." Boldface type indicates that group majorities are opposed to one another and that the difference is statistically significant at the 0.05 level. NA indicates that we did not have an oversample of this subgroup in the year that the question was asked.

*Statistically significant at the 0.05 level. Percentages rounded to nearest whole number.

Table A-2. Social Cleavages in Opinions on Education Issues among Teachers, 2011[a]

Issue/opinion	Teachers (1)	Parents (2)	Homeowners (3)	Affluent (4)	"Born again" (5)	Older (6)	Democrats (7)	Blacks (8)	Hispanics (9)
Teacher policy									
Use merit pay	−50*	9	−16*	NA	−2	−1	−6	NA	NA
Use merit tenure	−46*	8	−11	NA	−2	−2	−10	NA	NA
Allow flexible hiring	−28*	−2	−12	NA	3	16*†	−5	NA	NA
Eliminate tenure	−37*	13	5	NA	9†	11	−7	NA	NA
Teacher unions are harmful	−25*	10	9	NA	13*†	10	−38**	NA	NA
School choice									
Expand choice with universal vouchers	−27*	8	−16	NA	10	5	−18	NA	NA
Use government funds for means-tested vouchers	−24*	6	−22*	NA	16*	11†	−4	NA	NA
Allow charter schools	−17*	−1	−22	NA	8	1	−12	NA	NA
Allow tax credit–funded scholarships	−20*	5	0	NA	22**†	0	−9	NA	NA
Allow online courses	−9	5	−23**	NA	0	6	−11	NA	NA
Accountability									
Require annual testing	−24*	2	−6	NA	8	−1	−4	NA	NA
Use common standards/test	−12*	3	0	NA	−3	−8†	2	NA	NA
Use test for grade promotion	−15*	−13**	−1	NA	−3	12	−13*	NA	NA
Require graduation test	−10*	−3	6	NA	5	4	−14**	NA	NA

	(1)								
Taxes and spending									
Increase spending	6	-9†	NA	-7	NA	-3	-22**	27**	NA
Raise taxes	14*	-1	NA	-20*	NA	-11	-24**	26**	NA
Raise teacher pay	26*	3	NA	-18**	NA	1	-37**†	20**	NA
Increase teachers' share of benefit costs	-37*	4	NA	2	NA	0	28**	-8	NA
Cultural issues									
Allow single-sex schools	12*	-4	NA	-9	NA	13*	10	-15	NA
Grant principal final disciplinary authority	16*	3†	NA	-2	NA	1	-18**†	-4	NA
Allow silent prayer	-11*	8	NA	3	NA	**52**†	-8†	-46**†	NA
Diversity									
Use family income to assign students	0	-13**	NA	-14	NA	-15**†	-7	**29****	**NA**
Separate classes for disturbed students	2	-7	NA	-32**†	NA	17**†	22**	-7	**NA**

a. Column 1 shows the difference between teachers and the general public. All other columns show the differences in opinion between the indicated group and another group within the teaching profession. African Americans and Hispanics are each contrasted with whites. Democrats are contrasted with Republicans (partisan leaners excluded). "Older" refers to the oldest third (age 56 or older) contrasted with the youngest third (age 41 or younger). All other categories are the identified group contrasted with the remainder of teachers. Evangelicals are those who identified themselves as "born again." Boldface type indicates that group majorities are opposed to one another and that the difference is statistically significant. The statistical significance of differences between teachers and the general public was calculated with the general public defined as non-teachers (not shown); if teachers are included, as in table A-1, results vary by a trivial amount (usually, by 1 or 2 percentage points). NA indicates an insufficient number of observations to permit precise analysis. Percentages rounded to nearest whole number.

** Statistically significant at the 0.05 level; * statistically significant at the 0.10 level.

† Subgroup difference among teachers is statistically significantly different from the subgroup difference among the general public.

Selected Survey Questions, 2007–13

THE FOLLOWING ARE the survey questions that generated the responses analyzed in this book.

From the 2007 Survey

1a. Based on your best guess, what is the average amount of money spent each year for a child in public schools in your school district?

1b. Individual student costs go toward teacher and administrator salaries, building construction and maintenance, extracurricular activities, transportation, etc. Based on your best guess, what is the average amount of money spent each year for a child in public schools in your school district?

2. Based on your best guess, what is the average annual salary of a public school teacher in your state?

From the 2008 Survey

1. Students are often given the grades A, B, C, D, and Fail to denote the quality of their work. Suppose the public schools themselves were graded in the same way. What grade would you give the public schools in the nation as a whole?

2. How about the public schools in your local community? What grade would you give the public schools here?

3. How about the post offices in your local community? What grade would you give the post office here?

4. How about the police force in your local community? What grade would you give the police force here?

5a. According to the most recent information available, in your district $[current spending level] is being spent each year per child attending public schools. Do you think that government funding for public schools in your district should increase, decrease, or stay about the same?

5b. Do you think that government funding for public schools in your district should increase, decrease, or stay about the same?

6. If more money were spent on public schools in your district, how confident are you that students would learn more?

7a. According to the most recent information available, teachers in your state are paid an average annual salary of $[current average salary]. Do you think that teacher salaries at your local schools should increase, decrease, or stay about the same?

7b. Do you think that teacher salaries at your local schools should increase, decrease, or stay about the same?

8a. Many states permit the formation of charter schools, which are publicly funded but are not managed by the local school board. These schools are expected to meet promised objectives, but are exempt from many state regulations. Do you support or oppose the formation of charter schools?

8b. Many states permit the formation of charter schools, which are publicly funded but are not managed by the local school board. These schools are expected to meet promised objectives, but are exempt from many state regulations. However, these schools cannot charge tuition and they cannot provide religious instruction. Do you support or oppose the formation of charter schools?

8c. Many states permit the formation of charter schools, which are publicly funded but are not managed by the local school board. These schools are expected to meet promised objectives, but are exempt from many state regulations. However, these schools cannot choose among students who apply, they cannot charge tuition, and they cannot provide religious instruction. Do you support or oppose the formation of charter schools?

9. Some people say that principals should be the final authority on disciplinary matters. Other people say that students who have been suspended

from school have a right to appeal their punishment to the local school board. Which do you think is preferable?

10. In some public school districts, parents have requested that some time in each day be set aside for silent prayer and reflection. What do you think about this proposal?

From the 2009 Survey

1a. A 2006 government survey ranked the math skills of 15-year-olds in 29 industrialized countries. In this survey, the United States ranked 24th. Students are often given the grades A, B, C, D, and Fail to denote the quality of their work. Suppose the public schools themselves were graded in the same way. What grade would you give the public schools in the nation as a whole?

1b. According to the most recent available data, roughly 75 percent of 9th graders in U.S. public schools graduate from high school within four years. Students are often given the grades A, B, C, D, and Fail to denote the quality of their work. Suppose the public schools themselves were graded in the same way. What grade would you give the public schools in the nation as a whole?

From the 2010 Survey

1a. According to the most recent information available, in your district $[current spending level] is being spent each year per child attending public schools. Do you think that government funding for public schools in your district should increase, decrease, or stay about the same?

1b. Do you think that government funding for public schools in your district should increase, decrease, or stay about the same?

2. If more money were spent on public schools in your district, how confident are you that students would learn more?

3a. According to the most recent information available, teachers in your state are paid an average annual salary of $[current average salary]. Do you think that teacher salaries at your local schools should increase, decrease, or stay about the same?

3b. Do you think that teacher salaries at your local schools should increase, decrease, or stay about the same?

From the 2011 Survey

Evaluating Schools

1a. Students are often given the grades A, B, C, D, and Fail to denote the quality of their work. Suppose the public schools themselves were graded in the same way. What grade would you give the public schools in the nation as a whole?

1b. Students are often given the grades A, B, C, D, and Fail to denote the quality of their work. Suppose the public schools themselves were graded in the same way. What grade would you give the public schools in your community?

Personnel Policies

2a. Do you favor or oppose basing the salaries of teachers around the nation, in part, on their students' academic progress on state tests?

2b. Do you favor or oppose basing the salaries of teachers in your local schools, in part, on their students' academic progress on state tests?

3a. A proposal has been made that would require teachers across the country to demonstrate that their students are making adequate progress on state tests in order to receive tenure. Would you favor or oppose such a proposal?

3b. A proposal has been made that would require teachers in your local schools to demonstrate that their students are making adequate progress on state tests in order to receive tenure. Would you favor or oppose such a proposal?

4a. Do you favor or oppose allowing principals around the nation to hire college graduates who they believe will be effective in the classroom even if they do not have formal teaching credentials?

4b. Do you favor or oppose allowing principals in your local schools to hire college graduates who they believe will be effective in the classroom even if they do not have formal teaching credentials?

5a. Teachers with tenure cannot be dismissed unless a school district follows detailed procedures. Some say that tenure protects teachers from being fired for arbitrary reasons. Others say that it makes it too difficult to replace ineffective teachers. We want to know what you think of tenure. Do you favor or oppose offering tenure to teachers across the country?

5b. Teachers with tenure cannot be dismissed unless a school district follows detailed procedures. Some say that tenure protects teachers from being fired for arbitrary reasons. Others say that it makes it too difficult to replace ineffective teachers. We want to know what you think of tenure. Do you favor or oppose offering tenure to teachers in your local schools?

6a. Some people say that teacher unions are a stumbling block to school reform. Others say that unions fight for better schools and better teachers. What do you think? Do you think teacher unions have a generally positive effect on schools across the country, or do you think they have a generally negative effect?

6b. Some people say that teacher unions are a stumbling block to school reform. Others say that unions fight for better schools and better teachers. What do you think? Do you think teacher unions have a generally positive effect on your local schools, or do you think they have a generally negative effect?

School Choice Policies

7a. A proposal has been made that would give families with children in public schools a wider choice by allowing them to enroll their children in private schools instead, with government helping to pay the tuition. Would you favor or oppose this proposal?

7b. A proposal has been made that would use government funds to help pay the tuition of low-income students whose families would like them to attend private schools. Would you favor or oppose this proposal?

7c. A proposal has been made that would give families with children in your community's public schools a wider choice by allowing them to enroll their children in private schools instead, with government helping to pay the tuition. Would you favor or oppose this proposal?

7d. A proposal has been made that would use government funds to help pay the tuition of low-income students in your community whose families would like them to attend private schools. Would you favor or oppose this proposal?

8a. As you may know, many states permit the formation of charter schools, which are publicly funded but are not managed by the local school board. These schools are expected to meet promised objectives, but are exempt from many state regulations. Do you support or oppose the formation of charter schools?

8b. As you may know, many states permit the formation of charter schools, which are publicly funded but are not managed by the local school board. These schools are expected to meet promised objectives, but are exempt from many state regulations. Do you support or oppose the formation of charter schools in your community?

9a. Another proposal has been made to offer a tax credit for individual and corporate donations that pay for scholarships to help parents send their children to private schools. Would you favor or oppose such a proposal?

9b. Another proposal has been made to offer a tax credit for individual and corporate donations that pay for scholarships to help parents in your community send their children to private schools. Would you favor or oppose such a proposal?

10a. Another proposal has been made to allow high school students across the country to receive credit for state-approved courses taken over the Internet. Would you favor or oppose such a proposal?

10b. Another proposal has been made to allow high school students at your local high school to receive credit for state-approved courses taken over the Internet. Would you favor or oppose such a proposal?

Accountability

11. Some have proposed that the federal government continue to require that all students be tested in math and reading each year in grades 3–8 and once in high school. Do you support or oppose this proposal?

12. For holding schools accountable, should all state governments adopt the same set of educational standards and give the same tests in math, science, and reading? Or do you think that there should be different standards and tests in different states?

13a. In some states, students in certain grades must pass an exam before they are eligible to move on to the next grade. Do you support or oppose this requirement for students around the nation?

13b. In some states, students in certain grades must pass an exam before they are eligible to move on to the next grade. Do you support or oppose this requirement for students in your local schools?

14a. In some states, students must pass an exam before they are eligible to receive a high school diploma. Do you support or oppose this requirement for students nationwide?

14b. In some states, students must pass an exam before they are eligible to receive a high school diploma. Do you support or oppose this requirement for students in your local schools?

Taxes and Spending

15a. According to the most recent information available, $[current spending level] is being spent each year per child attending public schools in the United States. Do you think that government funding for public schools around the nation should increase, decrease, or stay about the same?

15b. Do you think that government funding for public schools around the nation should increase, decrease, or stay about the same?

15c. According to the most recent information available, in your district $[current spending level] is being spent each year per child attending public schools. Do you think that government funding for public schools in your district should increase, decrease, or stay about the same?

15d. Do you think that government funding for public schools in your district should increase, decrease, or stay about the same?

16a. Do you think that taxes to fund public schools around the nation should increase, decrease, or stay about the same?

16b. Do you think that local taxes to fund public schools in your district should increase, decrease, or stay about the same?

17a. According to the most recent information available, teachers in the United States are paid an average annual salary of $54,819. Do you think that these teacher salaries should increase, decrease, or stay about the same?

17b. Do you think that teacher salaries in the United States should increase, decrease, or stay about the same?

17c. According to the most recent information available, teachers in your state are paid an average annual salary of $[current average salary]. Do you think that teacher salaries at your local schools should increase, decrease, or stay about the same?

17d. Do you think that teacher salaries at your local schools should increase, decrease, or stay about the same?

18a. Some argue that teachers around the nation should be required to pay from their salaries 20 percent of the cost of their health care and pension benefits, with the government covering the remainder. What do you think of this proposal?

18b. Some argue that teachers in your local district should be required to pay from their salaries 20 percent of the cost of their health care and pension benefits, with the government covering the remainder. What do you think of this proposal?

Cultural Issues

19a. Some people have proposed that school districts around the nation offer parents the option of sending their child to an all-boys or all-girls school. What do you think about this proposal?

19b. Some people have proposed that your local school district offer parents the option of sending their child to an all-boys or all-girls school. What do you think about this proposal?

Diversity

20a. Should school districts across the country take the family income of students into account when assigning students to schools in order to ensure that each school has a mix of students from different backgrounds?

20b. Should your local school district take the family income of students into account when assigning students to schools in order to ensure that each school has a mix of students from different backgrounds?

21a. Some people say that students who have been diagnosed with emotional and behavioral disabilities should be taught in regular classrooms with other students. Other people say that these students should be taught in separate settings at the school. What do you think should be done with students around the nation who have emotional and behavioral disabilities?

21a. Some people say that students who have been diagnosed with emotional and behavioral disabilities should be taught in regular classrooms with other students. Other people say that these students should be taught in separate settings at the school. What do you think should be done with students in your local schools who have emotional and behavioral disabilities?

From the 2012 Survey

1. Based on your best guess, what is the average amount of money spent each year for a child in public schools in your school district?

2a. As it turns out, according to the most recent information available, $[current spending level] is being spent each year per child attending public schools in your district. Do you think that government funding for public schools in your district should increase, decrease, or stay about the same?

2b. Do you think that government funding for public schools in your district should increase, decrease, or stay about the same?

2c. As it turns out, according to the most recent information available, $[current spending level] is being spent each year per child attending public schools in your district. Do you think that taxes to fund public schools should increase, decrease, or stay about the same?

2d. Do you think that taxes to fund public schools should increase, decrease, or stay about the same?

3. Based on your best guess, what is the average annual salary of a public school teacher in your state?

4a. As it turns out, teachers in your state are paid an average annual salary of $[current average salary]. Do you think that teacher salaries should increase, decrease, or stay about the same?

4b. Do you think that teacher salaries should increase, decrease, or stay about the same?

5. A 2009 government survey ranked the math skills of 15-year-olds in 34 industrialized countries. What is your best guess of where American 15-year-olds ranked on this test?

6. What is your best guess as to the percentage of students in U.S. public school who graduate from high school within four years of entering 9th grade?

7. To the best of your knowledge, can charter schools hold religious services?

8. To the best of your knowledge, can charter schools charge tuition?

9. In general, do charter schools receive more, less, or the same amount of government funds for each student enrolled than do traditional public schools?

10. To the best of your knowledge, when more students apply to a charter school than there are spaces available, can the school pick the students they want or must they hold a lottery?

11. To the best of your knowledge, is there a charter school in your local school district?

From the 2013 Survey

Introduction a: Before you complete the rest of this survey, we want to provide you with some information about the performance of students in your local schools that may be of interest. A recent study compared the math test scores of students in your local school districts to the test scores of students across the United States. The study showed that students in your district perform at the [Xth] percentile of all students in the United States. This means that the average public school student in your district scores higher than [X] percent of American students and lower than [100-X] percent of American students. [This information remains available throughout the entire survey].

Introduction b: Before you complete the rest of this survey, we want to provide you with some information about the performance of students in your local schools that may be of interest. A recent study compared the math test scores of students in your local school districts to the test scores of students across the entire state. The study showed that students in your district perform at the [Xth] percentile of students in the state of [insert state name]. This means that the average public school student in the district scores higher than [X] percent of students in [insert state name] and lower than [100-X] percent of students in [insert state name]. [This information remains available throughout the entire survey].

Introduction c: [No information provided].

1. Students are often given the grades A, B, C, D, and Fail to denote the quality of their work. Suppose the public schools themselves were graded in the same way. What grade would you give the public schools in the nation as a whole?

2. Now about the public schools in your community? What grade would you give them?

3. Let's consider the public schools in your community once again. Some schools are good at teaching some students, but not so good at teaching other students. In your view, how well are the public schools in your community attending to the needs of the most talented students?

4. And what about the least talented students? How well are the public schools in your community attending to the needs of the least talented students?

5a. As it turns out, according to the most recent information available, $[current value] is being spent each year per child attending public schools in your district. Do you think that government funding for public schools in your district should increase, decrease, or stay about the same?

5b. Do you think that government funding for public schools in your district should increase, decrease, or stay about the same?

6. As you may know, many states permit the formation of charter schools, which are publicly funded but are not managed by the local school board. These schools are expected to meet promised objectives, but are exempt from many state regulations. Do you support or oppose the formation of charter schools?

7. In some parts of the country, a majority of parents whose children attend a low-performing traditional public school can sign a petition requiring the district to convert the school into a charter. What do you think of this policy?

8a. A proposal has been made that would give families with children in public schools a wider choice by allowing them to enroll their children in private schools instead, with government helping to pay the tuition. Would you favor or oppose this proposal?

8b. A proposal has been made that would use government funds to pay the tuition of low-income students who choose to attend private schools. Would you favor or oppose this proposal?

9. In some states, students must pass an exam before they are eligible to receive a high school diploma. Do you support or oppose this requirement?

10. In some states, third-grade students are required to pass the state's reading test to be eligible to move on to the fourth grade. Do you support or oppose this requirement for students?

11a. Do you think that public school teacher salaries in your state should increase, decrease, or stay about the same?

11b. As it turns out, public school teachers in your state receive, on average, salaries of $[current value]. In your view, should their salaries increase, decrease, or stay about the same?

12. How much trust and confidence do you have in public school teachers?

13. Teachers with tenure cannot be dismissed unless a school district follows detailed procedures. Some say that tenure protects teachers from being fired for arbitrary reasons. Others say that it makes it too difficult to replace ineffective teachers. We want to know what you think of tenure. Do you favor or oppose offering tenure to teachers?

14. Some people say that teacher unions are a stumbling block to school reform. Others say that unions fight for better schools and better teachers. What do you think? Do you think teacher unions have a generally positive effect on schools, or do you think they have a generally negative effect?

15. As you may know, all states are currently deciding whether or not to adopt the Common Core standards in reading and math. If adopted, these standards would be used to hold the state's schools accountable for their performance. Do you support or oppose the adoption of the Common Core standards in your state?

Detailed Responses to Questions in Tables 2-2 and A-1

TABLES 2-2 AND A-1 combine those who select the "completely" and "somewhat" favor response option as well as those who select the "completely" and "somewhat" oppose option. It also excludes those who select the "neither favor nor oppose" option. Following is the percentage distribution across all categories:

Merit pay: "Do you favor or oppose basing the salaries of teachers around the nation, in part, on their students' academic progress on state tests?"

Response	Teachers	Non-teachers
Completely favor	5	14
Somewhat favor	9	34
Neither favor nor oppose	9	26
Somewhat oppose	23	18
Completely oppose	53	8

Each subgroup is weighted using sample weights for the total population. For complete results for teachers using the teacher oversample weights, see documentation at "Education Next, PEPG Survey, 2011 (http://educationnext.org/files/EN-PEPG_Complete_Polling_Results_2011.pdf).

Merit tenure: "A proposal has been made that would require teachers across the country to demonstrate that their students are making adequate progress on state tests in order to receive tenure. Would you favor or oppose such a proposal?"

Response	Teachers	Non-teachers
Completely favor	9	21
Somewhat favor	18	35
Neither favor nor oppose	9	26
Somewhat oppose	23	12
Completely oppose	42	6

Flexible hiring: "Do you favor or oppose allowing principals around the nation to hire college graduates who they believe will be effective in the classroom even if they do not have formal teaching credentials?"

Response	Teachers	Non-teachers
Completely favor	8	12
Somewhat favor	19	31
Neither favor nor oppose	9	26
Somewhat oppose	19	19
Completely oppose	44	11

Tenure: "Teachers with tenure cannot be dismissed unless a school district follows detailed procedures. Some say that tenure protects teachers from being fired for arbitrary reasons. Others say that it makes it too difficult to replace ineffective teachers. We want to know what you think of tenure. Do you favor or oppose offering tenure to teachers across the country?"

Response	Teachers	Non-teachers
Completely favor	29	5
Somewhat favor	29	15
Neither favor nor oppose	11	31
Somewhat oppose	19	30
Completely oppose	13	19

Unions: "Some people say that teacher unions are a stumbling block to school reform. Others say that unions fight for better schools and better teachers. What do you think? Do you think teacher unions have a generally positive effect on your local schools, or do you think they have a generally negative effect?"

Response	Teachers	Non-teachers
Very positive	28	7
Somewhat positive	28	21
Neither positive nor negative	16	34
Somewhat negative	16	23
Very negative	11	15

Vouchers 1: "A proposal has been made that would give families with children in public schools a wider choice by allowing them to enroll their children in private schools instead, with government helping to pay the tuition. Would you favor or oppose this proposal?"

Response	Teachers	Non-teachers
Completely favor	12	19
Somewhat favor	19	29
Neither favor nor oppose	16	26
Somewhat oppose	15	16
Completely oppose	37	10

Vouchers 2: "A proposal has been made that would use government funds to help pay the tuition of low-income students whose families would like them to attend private schools. Would you favor or oppose this proposal?"

Response	Teachers	Non-teachers
Completely favor	10	14
Somewhat favor	12	24
Neither favor nor oppose	15	23
Somewhat oppose	20	18
Completely oppose	42	20

Charter schools: "As you may know, many states permit the formation of charter schools, which are publicly funded but are not managed by the local school board. These schools are expected to meet promised objectives, but are exempt from many state regulations. Do you support or oppose the formation of charter schools?"

Response	Teachers	Non-teachers
Completely favor	11	16
Somewhat favor	35	27
Neither favor nor oppose	16	39
Somewhat oppose	16	11
Completely oppose	22	6

Tax credits: "Another proposal has been made to offer a tax credit for individual and corporate donations that pay for scholarships to help parents send their children to private schools. Would you favor or oppose such a proposal?"

Response	Teachers	Non-teachers
Completely favor	19	19
Somewhat favor	26	31
Neither favor nor oppose	14	29
Somewhat oppose	16	13
Completely oppose	26	8

Online courses: "Another proposal has been made to allow high school students across the country to receive credit for state-approved courses taken over the Internet. Would you favor or oppose such a proposal?"

Response	Teachers	Non-teachers
Completely favor	10	14
Somewhat favor	37	33
Neither favor nor oppose	17	27
Somewhat oppose	21	18
Completely oppose	16	8

Require testing: "Some have proposed that the federal government continue to require that all students be tested in math and reading each year in grades 3–8 and once in high school. Do you support or oppose this proposal?"

Response	Teachers	Non-teachers
Completely favor	18	36
Somewhat favor	39	36
Neither favor nor oppose	13	19
Somewhat oppose	17	6
Completely oppose	13	3

Common standards/tests: "For holding schools accountable, should all state governments adopt the same set of educational standards and give the same tests in math, science, and reading? Or do you think that there should be different standards and tests in different states?"

Response	Teachers	Non-teachers
One test and standard for all	60	72
Different in different states	21	19
No national or state tests	18	9

Test for grade promotion: "In some states, students in certain grades must pass an exam before they are eligible to move on to the next grade. Do you support or oppose this requirement for students around the nation?"

Response	Teachers	Non-teachers
Completely favor	25	33
Somewhat favor	36	38
Neither favor nor oppose	16	19
Somewhat oppose	14	7
Completely oppose	10	5

Graduation test: "In some states, students must pass an exam before they are eligible to receive a high school diploma. Do you support or oppose this requirement for students nationwide?"

Response	Teachers	Non-teachers
Completely favor	32	41
Somewhat favor	35	31
Neither favor nor oppose	12	16
Somewhat oppose	14	7
Completely oppose	7	5

Spending: "Do you think that government funding for public schools in your district should increase, decrease, or stay about the same?"

Response	Teachers	Non-teachers
Greatly increase	25	16
Increase	44	43
Stay about the same	25	34
Decrease	6	5
Greatly decrease	0	3

Taxes: "Do you think that taxes to fund public schools around the nation should increase, decrease, or stay about the same?"

Response	Teachers	Non-teachers
Greatly increase	15	6
Increase	34	29
Stay about the same	40	52
Decrease	7	10
Greatly decrease	4	4

Teacher salaries: "Do you think that teacher salaries in the United States should increase, decrease, or stay about the same?"

Response	Teachers	Non-teachers
Greatly increase	37	14
Increase	43	41
Stay about the same	19	40
Decrease	1	5
Greatly decrease	1	2

Benefit costs: "Some argue that teachers around the nation should be required to pay from their salaries 20 percent of the cost of their health care and pension benefits, with the government covering the remainder. What do you think of this proposal?"

Response	Teachers	Non-teachers
Completely favor	8	15
Somewhat favor	15	28
Neither favor nor oppose	20	33
Somewhat oppose	20	14
Completely oppose	37	9

Single-sex schools: "Some people have proposed that school districts around the nation offer parents the option of sending their child to an all-boys or all-girls school. What do you think about this proposal?"

Response	Teachers	Non-teachers
Completely favor	16	12
Somewhat favor	32	22
Neither favor nor oppose	33	43
Somewhat oppose	11	14
Completely oppose	9	9

Income-based integration: "Should school districts across the country take the family income of students into account when assigning students to schools in order to ensure that each school has a mix of students from different backgrounds?"

Response	Teachers	Non-teachers
Definitely	9	7
Probably	21	17
Not sure	19	34
Probably not	26	19
Definitely not	25	23

Separate classes for students with disabilities: "Some people say that students who have been diagnosed with emotional and behavioral disabilities should be taught in regular classrooms with other students. Other people say that these students should be taught in separate settings at the school. What do you think should be done with students around the nation who have emotional and behavioral disabilities?"

Response	Teachers	Non-teachers
Completely favor teaching in regular class	9	7
Somewhat favor teaching in regular class	22	20
Neither favor nor oppose	9	24
Somewhat oppose teaching in regular class	42	33
Completely oppose teaching in regular class	18	16

Principal's authority: "Some people say that principals should be the final authority on disciplinary matters. Other people say that students who have been suspended from school have a right to appeal their punishment to the local school board. Which do you think is preferable?"

Response	Teachers	Non-teachers
Principals should be final authority	57	40
Right to appeal	43	60

Silent prayer: "In some public school districts, parents have requested that some time in each day be set aside for silent prayer and reflection. What do you think about this proposal?"

Response	Teachers	Non-teachers
Completely favor	28	34
Somewhat favor	16	16
Neither favor nor oppose	25	28
Somewhat oppose	11	8
Completely oppose	21	14

Note to Reader

THE MATERIAL IN this volume develops and extends material published in the following articles:

William G. Howell, Martin R. West, and Paul E. Peterson, "What Americans Think about Their Schools: The 2007 *Education Next*–PEPG Survey," *Education Next*, vol. 7, no. 4 (Fall 2007), pp. 12–26.

William G. Howell and Martin R. West, "Is the Price Right? Probing Americans' Knowledge of School Spending," *Education Next*, vol. 8, no. 3 (Summer 2008), pp. 36–41.

William G. Howell, Martin R. West, and Paul E. Peterson, "The 2008 *Education Next*-PEPG Survey of Public Opinion: Americans Think Less of Their Schools than of Their Police Departments and Post Offices," *Education Next*, vol. 8, no. 4 (Fall 2008), pp. 12–26.

William G. Howell and Martin R. West, "Educating the Public: How Information Affects Americans' Support for School Spending and Charter Schools," *Education Next*, vol. 9, no. 3 (Summer 2009), pp. 40–47.

William G. Howell, Martin R. West, and Paul E. Peterson, "The Persuadable Public: The 2009 *Education Next*-PEPG Survey Asks If Information Changes Minds about School Reform," *Education Next*, vol. 9, no. 4 (Fall 2009), pp. 20–29.

William G. Howell, Paul E. Peterson, and Martin R. West, "Meeting of the Minds: The 2010 *EdNext*-PEPG Survey Shows That, on Many Education Reform Issues, Democrats and Republicans Hardly Disagree," *Education Next*, vol. 11, no. 1 (Winter 2011), pp. 20–31.

William G. Howell, Martin R. West, and Paul E. Peterson, "The Public Weighs In on School Reform: Intense Controversies Do Not Alter

Public Thinking, but Teachers Differ More Sharply than Ever," *Education Next*, vol. 11, no. 4 (Fall 2011), pp. 10–22.

Martin R. West, Michael Henderson, and Paul E. Peterson, "The Education Iron Triangle," *The Forum*, vol. 10, no. 1 (2012).

William G. Howell, Martin R. West, and Paul E. Peterson, "Reform Agenda Gains Strength: The 2012 *EdNext*–PEPG Survey Finds Hispanics Give Schools Higher Grade than Others Do," *Education Next*, vol. 13, no. 4 (Winter 2013), pp. 8–19.

Notes

Chapter One

1. Ben Goldberger, "Karen Lewis: Street Fighter," *Chicago Magazine*, November 2012 (www.chicagomag.com/Chicago-Magazine/November-2012/Karen-Lewis-Street-Fighter/).

2. Ibid.

3. Paul E. Peterson, *School Politics Chicago Style* (University of Chicago Press, 1976).

4. Paul E. Peterson and Martin R. West, *No Child Left Behind?* (Brookings, 2002).

5. Paul E. Peterson and others, "Globally Challenged: Are U. S. Students Ready to Compete?" (Harvard Program on Education Policy and Governance, Harvard Kennedy School, 2011).

6. Goldberger, "Karen Lewis: Street Fighter."

7. Gallup, 42nd Annual Phi Delta Kappa/Gallup Poll of the Public's Attitudes toward the Public Schools (www.gallup.com/poll/142661/phi-delta-kappa-gallup-poll-2010.aspx).

8. Stacey Teicher Khadaroo, "Karen Lewis: Fiery Chicago Teachers Union Chief Takes on Wrath of Rahm," *Christian Science Monitor*, September 14, 2012.

9. For an early political analysis that gave full attention to both racial and teacher union politics, see Peterson, *School Politics Chicago Style*. For a recent analysis of union power, see Frederick Hess and Martin West, "A Better Bargain" (Harvard Program on Education Policy and Governance, Harvard Kennedy School, 2006) (www.hks.harvard.edu/pepg/PDF/Papers/BetterBargain.pdf). For recent work that focuses on teacher union politics, see Terry Moe, *Special Interest* (Brookings, 2011).

10. Regina A. Corso, "Prestige of 23 Professions and Occupations," *Harris Poll* 86, Harris Interactive, August 4, 2009.

11. Jeffrey R. Henig and others, *The Color of School Reform: Race, Politics, and the Challenge of Urban Education* (Princeton University Press, 2001); Howell S. Braun, *"Brown" in Baltimore: School Desegregation and the Limits of Liberalism* (Cornell University Press, 2010); William G. Howell and Paul E. Peterson, *The Education Gap* (Brookings, 2002); Jonathan Kozol, *The Shame of the Nation: The Restoration of Apartheid Schooling in America* (New York, N.Y.: Three Rivers Press, 2005).

12. See appendix A for details concerning survey design and administration.

13. Additional documentation, including initial reports and the full distribution of responses to questions from each survey, is available at the *EdNext* website (www. educationnext.org).

Chapter Two

1. Raj Chetty, John N. Friedman, and Jonah E. Rockoff, "The Long-Term Impacts of Teachers: Teacher Value-Added and Student Outcomes in Adulthood," Working Paper 17699 (Cambridge, Mass.: National Bureau of Economic Research, 2011). Also see Eric A. Hanushek and Steven G. Rivkin, "Generalizations about Using Value-Added Measures of Teacher Quality," *American Economic Review*, vol. 100, no. 2 (May 2010), pp. 267–71.

2. Frederick Hess and Martin West, "A Better Bargain" (Harvard Program on Education Policy and Governance, Harvard Kennedy School, 2006) (www.hks.harvard. edu/pepg/PDF/Papers/BetterBargain.pdf).

3. Kate Walsh, "Steps That Congress Can Take to Improve Teacher Quality—Without Overstepping Its Bounds" (Fordham Foundation Report, April 2007). Citations to research on the topics mentioned in this paragraph can be found in Paul E. Peterson, *Saving Schools: From Horace Mann to Virtual Learning* (Harvard University Press, 2010), pp. 293–94.

4. Stacey Teicher Khadaroo, "Karen Lewis: Fiery Chicago Teachers Union Chief Takes on Wrath of Rahm," *Christian Science Monitor,* September 14, 2012 (www.cs monitor.com/USA/Education/2012/0914/Karen-Lewis-Fiery-Chicago-Teachers-Union-chief-takes-on-wrath-of-Rahm-video).

5. Karen Lewis, "Why We're Striking in Chicago," *The Independent,* September 10, 2012.

6. As defined here, the general public excludes teachers, so in effect we are comparing teacher opinion to the opinion of all those who are not public school teachers.

7. Questions on spending, taxes, teacher salaries, common standards, and principals' discretion in disciplinary matters do not include a "neither favor nor oppose" response option, but on the remaining questions a considerable number of respondents take a neutral position. Among the general population, this share ranges from 19 percent on the question of whether the federal government should require testing to 42 percent on the question of single-sex schools. The results, therefore, speak only to the share of the population who chose a side on these issues. The advantage of excluding the neutral position, a common approach in the study of political opinions, is that it allows us to capture the level of support in relation to the level of opposition among any subgroup. Consider a hypothetical example in which 60 percent of teachers and the general public favor a policy, but the groups differ in their level of opposition, 35 percent among teachers and 10 percent among the general public, with the balance in each group taking the neutral position. The two groups express the same level of support, but the distribution of opinion is quite different. Our approach allows us to capture in a single number both the amount of support and the amount of opposition within a group.

One concern may be that we overstate the extent to which teachers and the general public disagree. While our approach produces larger estimated differences than when neutral responses remain, in no case do we identify statistically significant differences between these groups that are not also observable when all response options are used. Further, each issue where we identify a difference of opinion pitting a majority of teachers against a majority of the general public also shows differences between majorities (or, in some cases, pluralities) when the neutral responses are included. The distribution of responses across the full set of response options for both teachers and the general public can be found in appendix C. Finally, it is worth noting that the propensity to take the neutral position varies across subgroups, with teachers typically the least likely to express a neutral position. The average proportion of neutral responses across questions is 27 percent for the general population but only 15 percent for teachers. In chapter 5, we discuss further the difference between the percentage of teachers and the percentage of the public that took the neutral position on these issues.

8. Our analytical strategy is discussed in further detail in appendix A.

9. Stuart Buck and Jay P. Greene, "Blocked, Diluted, and Co-opted," *Education Next*, vol. 11, no. 2 (Spring 2011), pp. 26–31.

10. Milton Friedman, "The Role of Government in Education," in *Economics and the Public Interest*, edited by Robert Solo (Rutgers University Press, 1955).

11. National Education Association, "NEA Policy on Charter Schools: Adopted by the 2001 Representative Assembly" (www.nea.org).

12. Ben Goldberger, "Karen Lewis: Street Fighter," *Chicago Magazine*, November 2012.

13. "CTU 'Stand Up to the Fat Cats' Video Mocks Chicago Mayor, Education Reformers," *Huffington Post: Education*, December 11, 2012 (www.huffingtonpost.com/2012/12/11/ctu-stand-up-to-the-fat-cats_n_2277162.html).

14. Diane Ravitch, *The Death and Life of the Great American School System* (Basic Books, 2010), p. 145.

15. Ibid., p. 227.

16. Paul E. Peterson and Martin R. West, *No Child Left Behind? The Politics and Practice of School Accountability* (Brookings, 2003), chapters 1–5.

17. Jennifer Hochschild, "Rethinking Accountability Politics," in *No Child Left Behind?*, edited by Peterson and West, p. 112.

18. Lewis, "Why We're Striking in Chicago."

19. Ravitch, *The Death and Life of the Great American School System*, pp. 110–11.

20. This question has no neutral option. See appendix C.

21. Open letter from Diane Shust and Randall Moody, National Education Association, to Kenneth L. Marcus, Assistant Secretary for Civil Rights, U.S. Department of Education, April 23, 2004 (www.ncwge.org/documents/comments_NEA.pdf) .

22. Michael Broihier, "Woods OKs Teacher Led Prayer, Then Recants," *Kentucky News*, August 7, 2008 (http://articles.centralkynews.com/2008-08-07/news/2491 3671_1_public-school-teachers-teachers-and-school-district-student-prayer).

23. Richard Arum, *Judging School Discipline* (Harvard University Press, 2003).

24. Mary Ellen Flannery, "NEA Urges Supreme Court to Uphold Diversity Programs in College Admissions," *NEA Today*, October 10, 2012.

25. The federal Individuals with Disabilities Education Act (IDEA) identifies emotional and behavior disabilities as "emotional disturbance," defined as "a condition exhibiting one or more of the following characteristics over a long period of time and to a marked degree that adversely affects a child's educational performance: (a) An inability to learn that cannot be explained by intellectual, sensory, or health factors; (B) An inability to build or maintain satisfactory interpersonal relationships with peers and teachers; (C) Inappropriate types of behavior or feelings under normal circumstances; (D) A general pervasive mood of unhappiness or depression; and (E) A tendency to develop physical symptoms or fears associated with personal or school problems." Examples include but are not limited to anxiety disorders, bipolar disorder, and psychotic disorders.

26. Peterson, *Saving Schools*, p. 95.

27. More specifically, we standardized the five-point response scale for each issue (with higher values indicating more support) and regressed it on a binary indicator for employment as a teacher along with variables for respondent income, education, party identification, and evaluation of local public schools and separate binary indicators for gender, African American race, Hispanic ethnicity, region (South/non-South), homeownership, religious identity ("born again" or not), and parental status (of a child under the age of 18).

28. For ten items it was larger than 0.3 of a standard deviation of the response variable; for six it was larger than 0.5 of a standard deviation.

Chapter Three

1. Melissa Deckman, *School Board Battles: The Christian Right in Local Politics* (Georgetown, 2004). For a more general political analysis of cultural conflict in American politics, see Morris Fiorina, *Culture Wars: The Myth of a Polarized America*, 3rd ed. (Pearson, 2010).

2. Jonathan Kozol, *Savage Inequalities: Children in America's Schools* (Crown, 1991). Despite the title, Steven Brill, *Class Warfare: Inside the Fight to Fix America's Schools* (Simon & Schuster, 2011) focuses more on conflicts between teacher unions and the disadvantaged than between the rich and poor per se.

3. Michael B. Berkman and Eric Plutzer, *Ten Thousand Democracies: Politics and Public Opinion in America's School Districts* (Georgetown University Press, 2005). Their analysis shows less generational conflict that commonly thought.

4. William A. Fischel, *The Homevoter Hypothesis* (Harvard University Press, 2004); William A. Fischel, *Making the Grade: The Economic Evolution of American School Districts* (University of Chicago Press, 2009); James Poterba, "Demographic Structure and the Political Economy of Public Education," *Journal of Policy Analysis and Management*, vol. 16 (1997), pp. 48–66; James Poterba, "Demographic Change, Intergenerational Linkages, and Public Education," *American Economic Review*, vol. 88 (1998), pp. 315–20.

5. For a classic account, see Frank J. Munger and Richard F. Fenno Jr., *National Politics and Federal Aid to Education* (Syracuse University Press, 1962). Also see Elizabeth

H. DeBray, *Politics, Ideology, and Education* (Teachers College Press, 2006); Paul Manna, *School's In: Federalism and the National Education Agenda* (Georgetown University Press, 2006); Paul E. Peterson and Martin R. West, eds., *No Child Left Behind? The Politics and Practice of School Reform* (Brookings, 2003).

6. Jeffrey R. Henig and others, *The Color of School Reform: Race, Politics, and the Challenge of Urban Education* (Princeton University Press, 2001); Howell S. Braun, *"Brown" in Baltimore: School Desegregation and the Limits of Liberalism* (Cornell University Press, 2010); Jennifer Hochschild and Nathan Scovronick, *The American Dream and the Public Schools* (Oxford University Press, 2003); William G. Howell and Paul E. Peterson, *The Education Gap* (Brookings, 2002).

7. We also examined gender and regional (South versus other regions) divides and found them to be of lesser consequences than any of the others.

8. To make sure that we were not exaggerating these divides relative to others, we separately calculated the social divides by contrasting African Americans with all others, Hispanics with all others, and seniors with all others. When that was done, the racial and ethnic divides attenuated slightly, but the results were qualitatively the same as those reported. When the oldest are contrasted with all others, hardly any differences can be detected. We also carried out an analysis that included in our Democrat and Republican categories those independents who leaned toward one political party or another, thereby excluding only the 5 percent of the sample that insisted that it did not lean in either direction. Once again, the numerical results hardly budged; more results proved to be statistically significant, however, probably because sample size within categories increased. We do not control for other social background characteristics when discussing each social divide. Introducing such controls requires a theory as to what social characteristic is primary and which secondary. We know of no such theory. The one possible exception is the partisan cleavage, so we do discuss in a note below the pattern of results that we observe for the partisan divide, adjusted for all other social background characteristics.

9. The roughly 12 percent of families who send their children to private school or educate them at home do not have quite the same interests as other parents; nevertheless, we included all parents of school-age children because those who chose not to send their children to public schools might have taken public school quality into account when making their decision.

10. Jennifer Medina, "At California School, Parents Force an Overhaul," *New York Times*, December 7, 2010.

11. David Gergen and Ralph Reed, "Church and State," Public Broadcasting Service, Essays and Dialogues, transcript, June 6, 1966 (www.pbs.org/news hour/gergen/reed_6-6.html).

12. David Leonhardt, "Old vs. Young," Sunday Review, *New York Times*, June 22, 2012.

13. For examples, see the 2007–2010 Associated Press–Yahoo News Election Panel Study (http://surveys.ap.org/) and Gallup polling (www.gallup.com).

14. We excluded independents who lean toward one or another party.

15. When partisan differences are adjusted for social background characteristics, the differences between the parties narrow further. On three issues—using government

money for school vouchers, online learning, and allowing principals to hire teachers lacking state credentials—no statistically significant differences are detected. And differences, though statistically significant, are small on many other issues, including merit pay, awarding tenure only to meritorious teachers, mainstreaming, single-sex education, and all the questions concerning school and student accountability. After controls are introduced, what Republicans and Democrats disagree about is limited to standard partisan issues, such as taxes, spending, affirmative action, and the role of unions.

16. Classic works on this topic include Angus Campbell and others, *The American Voter* (Wiley, 1960); Philip Converse, "The Nature of Belief Systems in Mass Publics," in David Apter, *Ideology and Discontent* (Free Press, 1964), pp. 206–61; John Zaller, *The Nature and Origins of Mass Opinion* (Cambridge University Press, 1992).

17. Gallup Daily: Obama Job Approval (www.gallup.com/poll/113980/Gallup-Daily-Obama-Job-Approval.aspx).

Chapter Four

1. Between 1974 and 2008, 18 percent of the respondents, on average, gave the schools one of the two lowest grades in the PDK poll. For the years 2007 to 2011, that average was 17 percent.

2. The PDK poll percentages presented here ignore those who said that they did not know what grade to give the schools. The graph eliminates short-term variation that could be due to sampling error by showing running three-year averages. The *Ednext* surveys do not offer respondents the "Don't know" option; since the survey has been administered for only a few years, actual results are shown rather than three-year running averages. The two separate surveys for any one year usually differ by a margin that is no greater than what can be attributed to conventional sampling error, an indication that online and telephone surveys yield similar results.

3. Changes in question wording do not always fetch such strikingly different responses. For example, in 2010 we asked two randomly selected segments their opinion about charter schools in contrasting ways:

Version 1: "As you may know, many states permit the formation of charter schools, which are publicly funded but are not managed by the local school board. These schools are expected to meet promised objectives, but are exempt from many state regulations. Do you support or oppose the formation of charter schools?"

Version 2: "As may know, many states allow publicly authorized charter schools. These schools receive most of their funding from the government but they are privately managed. Do you support or oppose the formation of charter schools?"

Notice that while both questions accurately describe charter schools, version 1 emphasizes "exemption from state regulations," while version 2 talks about "privately managed" schools. We expected more opposition to "privately managed" schools than to schools that were "exempt from state regulations." But despite the difference in wording, the same percentage—44 percent—say that they support charter schools, no matter which question is asked. Those opposed shift only insignificantly—from 19 percent to 22 percent. Those taking a neutral position, saying they neither supported nor opposed charters, remain at about 35 percent.

4. Richard F. Fenno, *Home Style: House Members in Their Districts* (Little, Brown, 1978).

5. Information is available for only two years, 2008 and 2011.

Chapter Five

1. Paul E. Peterson, *Saving Schools: From Horace Mann to Virtual Learning* (Harvard University Press, 2011), chapter 2.

2. For example, the websites Education.com and Greatschools.org provide test-score information for schools throughout the United States.

3. Per-pupil expenditures vary widely from one district to another—from a minimum of $5,644 to a maximum of $24,939 for the 2004–05 school year in the districts included in our sample.

4. We were able to provide respondents with this information because we knew their place of residence prior to administering the survey (see appendix A for details).

5. In other words, opinion shifts by 18 percentage points (or 32 percent) when information is provided. Percentage change is the simple difference between the groups. Percent change is that percentage change divided by the initial percentage. Percent changes are larger if the initial percentage is smaller. For example, a hypothetical shift in opinion favoring funding of a program to shoot asteroids in outer space from 5 percent to 10 percent would be a 100 percent change, even though it would be only a 5 percentage-point change. Both statistics are useful; percentage-point change identifies actual shifts, while percent change takes into account the initial distribution of opinion. To avoid confusion, we report the more conservative percentage-point change in the text but provide in the notes the percent change when this way of calculating informational impact is of interest.

6. That is a drop of 27 percent.

7. That is a remarkable 60 percent change in the distribution of public opinion.

8. That constitutes a 41 percent change in the distribution of teacher opinion.

9. Teacher salaries range from a low of $34,039 in South Dakota to a high of $57,760 in Alaska. See appendix A for the methodology that we use to obtain public information concerning teacher salaries.

10. Neither the AFT nor the federal government provides information on teacher salaries by school district.

11. The numbers are averages for the three years: 2008, 2009, and 2011. It is a 24 percent decrease.

12. That is a 56 percent decline.

13. While some 83 percent of the uninformed teachers favor higher salaries, 76 percent of those who were informed did so.

14. On the median issue, 27 percent of the public but just 15 percent of teachers took the neutral position.

15. The question was asked in 2012.

16. Since we asked only about these two topics in 2007, they are the only items reported in table 5-2 for which change over time can be estimated.

17. In the 2008 survey, 27 percent of respondents identified themselves as liberal, 34 percent as conservative, and 39 percent as moderate.

18. As discussed in chapter 3 (see table 3-1), we conducted a survey experiment in which half of the respondents were told that Obama supported charters; that information increased support for charters, particularly among groups in which large majorities voted for him the previous year.

19. Chris Chapman, Jennifer Lair, and Angelina Kewal Ramani, *Trends in High School Dropout and Completion Rates in the United States,* 1972–2008, Compendium Report, NCES 2011-012 (U.S. Department of Education, National Center for Education Statistics, December 2010), p. 13 (nces.ed.gov/pubs2011/2011012.pdf). The graduation rate for the school year ending in 2010 was preliminarily estimated to be 78 percent, an estimate that is a major uptick from the year ending in 2008 and one that is subject to revision when data are completely analyzed. Robert Stillwell and Jennifer Sable, "Public School Graduates and Dropouts from the Common Core of Data, School Year 2009–2010: First Look (Provisional Data)" (U. S. Department of Education, National Center for Education Statistics, January 2013), table 3. According to the estimate by another national survey, the graduation rate in 2010 was 75 percent. "Diploma Counts 2013," Editorial Projects in Education Research Center, *Education Week,* 2013.

20. This discussion assumes that the sum of all local school district graduation rates equals the nation's graduation rate.

21. The percentage giving schools an "A" or "B" (on the traditional scale used to evaluate students) increased by just 2 percentage points and the percentage getting a "D" or "F" dropped by 1 percentage point. Since teachers were not included in the 2009 experiment, we do not know what impact information would have had on teacher assessments.

22. Marguerite Roza and Jon Fullerton, "Funding Phantom Students," *Education Next,* vol. 13, no. 3 (Summer 2013).

23. The National Center on Education Statistics in the U.S. Department of Education periodically administers the Schools and Staffing Survey, which collects information on teacher compensation by state. The most recent report was for the school year 2007–08. Selected states also participate in the Teacher Compensation Survey; the most recent report is for the 2006–07 school year.

Chapter Six

1. William G. Howell is a co-author of this chapter.

2. Arne Duncan, "Reauthorization of ESEA: Why We Can't Wait," Secretary of Education Arne Duncan's Remarks at the Monthly Stakeholders Meeting, September 24, 2009 (www.ed.gov/news/speeches/reauthorization-esea-why-we-cant-wait).

3. Lisa Fleicher and Stephanie Banchero, "National Test-Score Declines Are Likely," *Wall Street Journal,* August 6, 2013.

4. We realize, of course, that some within this group may have independently acquired knowledge about student performance from sources other than our survey questionnaire. The group is *uninformed*, therefore, only in the technical sense that they were not given specific items of information supplied to the other groups.

5. Recall that our measure of support is the share of respondents among those either supporting or opposing a proposition (that is, we exclude neutral respondents). In 2013 the percentage of respondents taking the neutral position was reduced significantly by the decision to place this response last among available alternatives instead of third (in the middle) as had been done in prior surveys. Comparisons between 2013 results and earlier ones should be made cautiously; we have made no such comparisons in this book.

6. Quoted in Valerie Strauss, "What Big Drop in New Standardized Test Scores Really Means," *Washington Post*, August 7, 2013.

Chapter Seven

1. Sarah Kate Kramer, "Tougher to Get Tenure: What Do the Teachers Think?," WNYC, July 28, 2011.

2. Richard Corliss, "*Waiting for 'Superman'*: Are Teachers the Problem?" *Time*, September 29, 2010.

3. "Christie Softens on Teachers, Blames Unions and Not Individuals," *The Record*, April 11, 2013.

4. Richard Lee Colvin, "Taking Back Teaching: Educators Organize to Influence Policy and Their Profession," *Education Next*, vol. 12, no. 2 (Spring 2012), pp. 23–28.

5. Ibid., p. 28.

6. Eighty-six percent of the teachers in our sample say that they hold a college degree, and virtually all have attended college for some length of time. That the percentage is not closer to 100 may be due to self-identification as teachers by paraprofessionals working in schools. Over 11 percent of all professional employees are instructional aides. It is also possible that some respondents made coding errors and that some older teachers did not have a college degree.

7. See appendix A for details of sample size and construction.

8. Consider, for example, differences between parents and the general public displayed in column 2 of tables A-1 and A-2. Overall, parent differences with the rest of the population are statistically significant for six issues, but only two are observed for teachers and the general population. Based on that result, it is tempting to conclude that the parent divide among teachers is less than in the public at large. But the difference may be due to the fact that we have only 145 observations of teachers who are parents, making it difficult to detect anything other than very large divides. Had we had more observations of teachers who were parents, we might have found that such teachers were more likely to think that unions are harmful and that tenure should be eliminated, as those cleavages are in double digits. Unfortunately, our sample size is not large enough to be sure.

9. In table A-2 we also report the homeowner, non-homeowner divide, but we do not find it of sufficient interest to discuss.

10. Jackie Mader, "Survey: Today's Teaching Force Is Less Experienced, More Open to Change," *HechingerEd* October 23, 2012 (http://hechingered.org/content/survey-todays-teaching-force-is-less-experienced-more-open-to-change_5719/). For the teacher survey, see Teach Plus, *Great Expectations: Teachers' Views on Elevating the Profession,*" 2012 (www.teachplus.org/uploads/Documents/1350917768_Teach%20Plus%20Great%20Expectations.pdf).

11. Admittedly, these numbers do not tell us whether the teaching profession is changing or whether the differences by age reported in table A-2 reflect differences between the opinions of those in the earlier years of their career and those near the end of it. Nor do we know whether any observed difference is due to differences between the kinds of individuals who remain in teaching over the long run and those who leave after a few years. One can provide definitive evidence on changes over time only by tracking teacher opinion from one year to the next. Generally speaking, we have found very little shift in teacher opinion over the course of the surveys that *Education Next* has conducted.

12. Even after we control for the demographic characteristics of our survey respondents, the differences between Democratic and Republican teachers on these issues are very close to the differences between Democrats and Republicans in general.

Chapter Eight

1. Paul E. Peterson, *Saving Schools: From Horace Mann to Virtual Learning* (Harvard University Press, 2010), pp. 105–07.

2. Mike Antonucci, "The Long Reach of Teachers Unions," *Education Next*, vol. 10, no. 4 (Fall 2010), pp. 24–31.

3. Clive Thomas and Ronald Hrebenar, "Interest Groups in the States," in *Politics in the American States*, 8th ed., edited by Virginia Gray and Russell L. Hanson (Washington: CQ Press, 2004), p. 119.

4. Philip Converse, "The Nature of Belief Systems in Mass Society," in *Ideology and Discontent*, edited by David E. Apter (New York: Free Press of Glencoe, 1964), pp. 206–61.

5. Benjamin Page and Robert Shapiro, *The Rational Public* (University of Chicago Press, 1992); James Stimson, *Public Opinion in America: Moods, Cycles, and Swings* (Boulder, Colo.: Westview, 1991).

6. Questions in 2013 are not comparable because the neutral category was placed last among available choices, reducing the percentages that chose that option; with a higher percentage of respondents taking a position on the issue, percentages can change even when public opinion has not.

7. Stanley Feldman, "Structure and Consistency in Public Opinion: The Role of Core Beliefs and Values," *American Journal of Public Opinion*, vol. 32 (1988), pp. 416–40; Stanley Feldman and John Zaller, "A Simple Theory of the Survey Response: Answering Questions versus Revealing Preferences," *American Journal of Political Science*, vol. 36 (1992), pp. 579–616.

8. George J. Stigler, "The Theory of Economic Regulation," *Bell Journal of Economic and Management Sciences*, vol. 2 (Spring 1971), pp. 3–21; Richard A. Posner, "Theories of Economic Regulation," *Bell Journal of Economic and Management Sciences*, vol. 5 (1974), p. 335; Jean-Jacques and Jean Tirole, "The Politics of Government Decision-Making: A Theory of Regulatory Capture," *Quarterly Journal of Economics*, vol. 106, no. 4 (1991), pp. 1089–127.

9. Marver H. Bernstein, *Regulating Business by Independent Commission* (Princeton University Press, 1955); Harold Seidman, *Politics, Position, and Power: The Dynamics of Federal Organization*, 2nd ed. (Oxford University Press, 1975).

10. Richard D. Stone, *The Interstate Commerce Commission and the Railroad Industry: A History of Regulatory Policy* (New York: Praeger, 1991).

11. Stephen Labaton, "Exemption Won in '97 Set Stage for Enron Woes," *New York Times*, January 23, 2002, p. A1.

12. Eric M. Johnson, "Seattle Teachers Boycotting Standardized Test Won't Be Punished," Reuters, April 1, 2013.

13. Steven Levitt and Brian Jacob, "To Catch a Cheat," *Education Next*, vol. 4, no. 1 (Winter 2004), pp. 68–75.

14. Paul E. Peterson and Carlos Lastra-Anadón, "State Standards Rise in Reading, Fall in Math," *Education Next*, vol. 10, no. 4 (Fall 2010), pp. 12–17.

15. William Howell, "One Child at a Time," *Education Next*, vol. 4, no. 3 (Summer 2004), pp. 26–31.

16. Sara Mead, "Easy Way Out: Restructured Usually Means Little Has Changed," *Education Next*, vol. 7, no. 1 (Winter 2007), 50-59.

17. Stuart Buck and Jay P. Greene, "Blocked, Diluted, and Co-opted: Interest Groups Wage War against Merit Pay," *Education Next*, vol. 11, no. 2 (Spring 2011), pp. 26–31.

18. Motoko Rich, "Education Chief Lets States Delay Use of Tests in Decisions about Teachers' Jobs," *New York Times*, June 18, 2013.

19. Martha Derthick and Paul Quirk, *The Politics of Deregulation* (Brookings, 1985); Robert Crandall and Jerry Ellig, *Economic Deregulation and Customer Choice* (George Mason University, 1997); Robert W. Poole Jr. and Viggo Butler, *Airline Deregulation: The Unfinished Revolution*, 1998 (http://cei.org/pdf/1451.pdf); Steven A. Morrison and Clifford Winston, "The Remaining Role for Government Policy in the Deregulated Airlines Industry," in *Regulation of Network Industries: What's Next?*, edited by Sam Peltzman and Clifford Winston (Washington, D. C.: AEI-Brookings Joint Center for Regulatory Studies, 2000).

20. Derthick and Quirk, *The Politics of Deregulation*.

21. See chapter 2 for the method we used to calculate public opinion.

22. Paul E. Peterson, "Teacher Unions, Mac the Knife, and Dollar Power," *Education Next*, January 11, 2012 (http://educationnext.org/teacher-unions-mac-the-knife-and-dollar-power/).

Index

ABOUT THE AUTHORS

Paul E. Peterson is the Henry Lee Shattuck Professor of Government and director of the Program on Education Policy and Governance, Harvard University. He is also editor-in-chief of *Education Next* and a senior fellow at the Hoover Institution.

Michael Henderson is assistant professor in the Department of Political Science, University of Mississippi.

Martin R. West is associate professor of education at the Harvard Graduate Schools of Education, deputy director of the Program on Education Policy and Governance, and nonresident senior fellow with the Brown Center on Education Policy, Brookings.